Achievement
TESTING

in U.S. Elementary and Secondary Schools

PETER LANG
New York • Washington, D.C./Baltimore • Bern
Frankfurt am Main • Berlin • Brussels • Vienna • Oxford

JOAN M. BAKER

Achievement
TESTING

in U.S. Elementary and Secondary Schools

PETER LANG

New York • Washington, D.C./Baltimore • Bern
Frankfurt am Main • Berlin • Brussels • Vienna • Oxford

Library of Congress Cataloging-in-Publication Data

Baker, Joan M. (Joan Maureen).
Achievement testing / Joan M. Baker.
p. cm.
Includes bibliographical references and index.
1. Achievement tests—United States. 2. Educational tests and measurements—
United States. I. Title.
LB3060.3.B35   371.26'2—dc22   2004027262
ISBN 0-8204-7631-5

Bibliographic information published by **Die Deutsche Bibliothek**.
Die Deutsche Bibliothek lists this publication in the "Deutsche
Nationalbibliografie"; detailed bibliographic data is available
on the Internet at http://dnb.ddb.de/.

Cover design by Dutton & Sherman Design

The paper in this book meets the guidelines for permanence and durability
of the Committee on Production Guidelines for Book Longevity
of the Council of Library Resources.

 # Contents

Preface vii

Acknowledgments ix

Chapter One. Looking at the History of Testing 1

Chapter Two. Examining the Birth of the Achievement Tests—
    Informal and Formal 11

Chapter Three. Exploring the Completion of the
    Formal Achievement Test 23

Chapter Four. Peering Through the Kaleidoscope of Tests
    and Their Uses and Result 35

Chapter Five. Viewing Achievement Tests Through the Eyes
    of Professional Organizations and Other Stakeholders 49

Chapter Six. Analyzing the Qualities of Fair Assessments 69

Chapter Seven. Visiting Achievement Test Misuses and Abuses 81

Chapter Eight. Accepting Achievement Tests As a Way of Life 109

Preface

The purpose of this book is to provide an opportunity for new educators—beginning teachers—and parents to view and reflect on the various aspects of school achievement testing. The book takes a glimpse into past and present achievement testing practices, including the different types of achievement testing, uses and abuses of achievement tests, and the factors that should be taken into consideration in developing fair achievement tests. The positions of many stakeholders—educators, researchers, theorists, and parents—are briefly viewed. Finally, the necessity of using various types of tests to improve teaching and learning is explored.

The topics are presented so that you will have a clear overview of them. The presentations will give you background information which will help in the understanding of basic aspects of testing. The background information should help you, the new educator or parent, if you choose or are required to read and digest advanced technical manuals, books, and journals on the subject of school achievement testing.

Included in the book will be brief discussions of the following topics. (The word *brief* is stressed because in more advanced technical books, a number of the chapters or even an entire book may be devoted to any one of the topics presented here.)

The topics discussed in this book are:

- Looking at the history of testing
- Examining the birth of achievement tests—formal and informal
- Exploring the completion of the formal achievement test
- Peering through the kaleidoscope of tests and their uses
- Viewing achievement tests through the eyes of professional organizations and other stakeholders
- Analyzing standards for a fair test
- Visiting test misuses and abuses
- Accepting achievement tests as a way of life

Achievement testing in various forms has always been part of school evaluation. It will continue to be a valuable tool of the school. However, the accuracy and the appropriateness of tests are extremely important considerations. Equally as important is the understanding that any test must be used with many other measures when evaluating the student's performance. In medicine, the doctor uses many different kinds of tests to get a whole picture of his/her patient. Like the doctor, the school must use many different measures to get a holistic view of the student's academic performance.

Additionally, it is hoped that through this concise exploration of school testing, that you—whether a new educator or a parent—will see it as a part of the whole performance picture of a student. Far from giving a whole picture, tests that are inaccurate, inappropriate, or misused as a sole measure in the doctor's hands can lead to the patient's injury or death. Such tests in the hands of the teacher or school system can lead to the academic injury or failure of the student. The goal in each profession is to get a comprehensive view of the patient or student as the case may be.

Acknowledgments

I wish to express my gratitude to the following publishers and education organizations who gave me permission to include a portion of their copyrighted material in my book. I am especially grateful to the education organizations, key education stakeholders, whose collective voices about learning, teaching, and achievement testing, found in their standards, spoke clearly about their positions in these areas.

The International Reading Association for excerpts from the following documents:

- *A Position Statement on Minimum Competencies in Reading:* Adopted by the Board of Directors of International Reading Association (1979), presented in *The Reading Teacher,* 33 (October 1979), 54–55.
- International Reading Associations/Task Force on Assessment (1994) *Standards for Assessment of Reading and Writing,* National Council of Teachers of English and International Reading Association, 33–37.
- International Reading Association, "Reading Scores Remain Flat." *Reading Today,* (December 2003/January 2004), 5.

The National Council of Teachers of Mathematics for excerpts from *Assessment Standards for Mathematics,* 1995, and *Principles and Standards for School Mathematics,* 2000.

The National Center for Improving Science Education for Improvement Goal 2 in "Active Assessment for Active Science," in *Expanding Student Assessment,* edited by

Vito Perrone, and The Association for Supervision and Curriculum Development. Alexandra, Virginia. 1991. p. 107.

The Association for Supervision and Curriculum Development for a quote from the editor of *Expanding Student Assessment* and for a quotation of Vito Perrone, editor, in *Expanding Student Assessment*.

The National Board of Educational Testing and Public Policy for quotations from *From Gatekeeper to Gateway: Transforming Testing in America,* pages 26 and 30.

National Council for Social Studies (NCSS) for NCSS's position statements in part or whole and portions of the standards of NCSS.

Wiley Publishing Company from Phillip Schlechty's *Schools for the 21ˢᵗ Century.*

Additionally, I would like to express my gratitude to Fedelma Ash for reading/reviewing this text with me. I am grateful to the multitude of students whom I taught at all levels—elementary, secondary, and higher education—my family, colleagues, and friends who inspired me to write this book. I am especially indebted to the faculty in the College of Education at Indiana University, Bloomington, who are stellar educators.

CHAPTER ONE

Looking at the History of Testing

Psychological testing (inclusive of school testing) is a relatively young branch of one of the youngest of the sciences.

ANNE ANASTASI

School testing is a way of looking at the performance of a student. This look at or examination of performance may take many different forms. These varied ways of looking at performance are examined throughout this book. This chapter begins with test practices from the early American schools. Many of these test practices affect today's schools, but new test practices have developed as a result of increased, diverse school populations, changed needs, and research findings

EARLY USE OF INFORMAL TESTS

In order to reflect on the past as far as school testing, it is necessary to revisit the history of American schools. And, to add to Anne Anastasi's (1976) statement in the book *Psychological Testing* at the beginning of this chapter, it is the formal test which is relatively new, not the informal test. (The formal test will be discussed in this chapter and throughout the book.) Informal tests—observation and teacher-made tests such as spelling tests, grammar tests, arithmetic tests, and essays and essay tests—were the primary tests in the early schools of America. Probably, these tests were adequate for the educational needs of the elite group of students in attendance in America's schools at that time. This elite group of students represented only a small proportion of America's school-age population. They were generally from the wealthy families. Unlike today's schools, the schools in the eighteenth and nineteenth centuries were not diverse.

Early schools reflected the culture of the country as they do today. Initially, it was the boys rather than the girls who were educated. The texts were the hornbook, primers, and religious material such as the Lord's Prayer and the Bible. In the late eighteenth century when the population was a little less than four million, the majority of families lived on farms. The father generally was in charge of socialization and education. Later, the mother assisted with the task of education. At the beginning of the Industrial Revolution, 80% of the families lived on farms. In these rural areas, teaching took place often in one-room schoolhouses, and commonly the teachers had finished four years of school beyond the elementary level. It is believed, however, that few students attended school. There was no compulsory education law. The school year ranged from 12 weeks to six months.

At the beginning of the twentieth century, only 22 percent of elementary-aged children were in attendance in elementary schools. Only 10 percent of the high-school-age students were in attendance in high schools according to Robert Zais (1976) in *Curriculum Principles and Foundations*. (Many children of working-class families of the eighteenth and nineteenth centuries provided the extra hands on the family farms. After the Industrial Revolution many poor children worked side by side with adults in the emerging factories. Black slave children and even most Black free children were legally excluded from school.) With the coming of each decade in the twentieth century, the American school population doubled. In the late twentieth century and now in the twenty-first century, almost all American school-age children are in school. With the inclusion of more and more children, the school population of today has become very diverse.

EARLY USE OF SUBJECTIVE TESTS

From the early schools came some of the test practices that still exist in today's schools. The use of the essay test or subjective test, where students respond to teacher-made questions by writing out their responses, was one of the test legacies from this period. Hopefully, these tests handed down from the past are different now because research has shown the following: In the subjective test the students' knowledge and their points of view flow together in their answers. Because of the mix of knowledge and students' points of view, at times there may be a number of answers that are correct. In evaluating the answers to the test questions, the teacher is not only influenced by his/her own point of view but by the prior academic experiences with the student writer and expectations of him or her. Probably the most critical limitation of the subjective test of the past and present is that it is often hard to grade and requires a great deal of the teacher's time. With the increase in the general school population and the diversity of the new students, these factors posed by the subjective tests became very important issues.

DEVELOPMENT OF OBJECTIVE TESTS

Probably the diverse nature of America's twentieth–century schools with the tremendous increase in population led educators to explore tests that would help to measure the difference in performance of the students in an objective way. A glimpse back to the late nineteenth century would show the birth of the objective tests. Such tests are called "objective" because there is one correct or best answer for a given question or item. This type of test is described more fully in the next paragraph. The first objective tests were designed to classify and train mentally retarded students. This is in direct contrast with today's school where almost all students take objective tests in standardized group testing situations and in some classroom testing. (Standardized tests will be discussed in the next chapter.)

What is the objective test? The objective test is an examination where the test items are usually in the form of a question or an incomplete statement. Usually three or four options are given as possible answer choices. One of the options is the correct or best answer. The student taking the test has to select the correct or best answer from the options. The test items—questions or problems—are called multiple choice. Because of the design of the multiple-choice items, unlike the subjective test mentioned previously, there is only one correct or best answer. An example of an objective question is:

1. *The first president of the United States was:*
   a. John Adams   b. Thomas Jefferson   c. George Washington

Personal points of view do not enter into the answer choice. Anyone grading the test should get the same score. In the beginning of the twentieth century psychologists used this format in designing intelligence tests, achievement tests, and other tests.

How and why did the objective test come into such popular use? There are a number of answers to this question. One reason that this test form came into popular use is that the format became readily available. It was found that it was relatively easy to design a test using this format. The fact that there was a single correct answer which could be recorded by having the student or test taker write or circle the number or letter preceding the answer made the test easy to score. Because there was only one correct answer, this meant that anyone with an answer key could correctly score the test. Early on, answer grids were developed to speed the grading process. With this grading process, there was a great saving of time. Additionally, scores of students could be easily compared. These were important considerations with the increase in the population of students in the twentieth-century schools. Today, when objective tests are used for school-wide testing, the machine-scorable sheets are generally used with older students so that they can be graded easily and quickly by machine.

STANDARDIZED TESTS

Anastasi describes the psychological test as " . . . essentially an objective and standardized measure of a sample of behavior." Standardized means that there is an exact way or standard by which the test is to be taken. In the standardized objective test, the qualities of the objective test mentioned above are combined with test-imposed standards. There are directions that should be read to or by each student taking the test. In many standardized tests, every student has the same time limit for completing the test. The tests are scored in the same way for each student. There is another important feature about a standardized test: it has been tested to see that it really assesses what the designer of the test says it measures before it is ever given to students who are to be evaluated by it. It has been checked for accuracy and general fairness of the questions for the students who are supposed to take the test. Students have participated in the testing of the test. (This will be discussed further in Chapter two.) Another very important concept in the Anastasi quotation is that any test is just a sample of behavior. This directly relates to the idea in the preface which says that any test is just a part of the whole performance of a student. The idea that a test is just a sample of behavior is a very important concept to remember.

The standardized objective test that Anastai mentions above is part of the school testing that most American students experience in their school life. Some students experience the standardized objective test at least one or more times each school year. The objective teacher-made test may be experienced many times a year, semester, or grading period. Because of frequent standardized testing experiences, the Education Testing Service (ETS) and the College Board are institutions that high school and college students are well acquainted with.

The establishment of the Educational Testing Service and the College Board early in the twentieth century foreshadowed the key roles that they would play in education. At first they had little power, but now with their publishing of the Scholastic Aptitude Test, the Advanced Placement Test, the Graduate Record Examination, the Praxis Examination, the College Level Examination Placement Program, and numerous other standardized tests, they are giants in education.

COMPARISON OF TEACHER-MADE AND STANDARDIZED TESTS

The teacher-made objective test, as its name implies, is usually a test containing multiple-choice questions. Sometimes the teacher-made objective test contains true-false test items, matching items, or fill-in-the-blank items as well. As with other classroom tests, it is designed by a teacher to evaluate the progress that students are making in learning the material presented in class from the textbook, class discussion, class projects, and other learning activities.

The newly developed standardized objective test and the teacher-made objective test have similarities and differences. The similarities are the format, the clear directions for taking the test, the ease of scoring. The differences are (1) in the planning time, (2) in the testing of the questions, directions, and scoring of the test items, and (3) in the initial administering of the new test to large segments of the age or grade appropriate student population nationally in not-for-student-academic-credit trials and then examining the results to determine the test reliability and validity. This difference discussed here represents the process of testing or evaluating the test itself. Technically, the testing of the test is called the validation. The initial evaluating or testing of the test occurs in the development of the standardized objective test, not the teacher-made test. The validation is done by test designers in research projects usually through large publishing houses. This process, including the not-for-student-academic-credit trials often takes two or more years. Only after the validation process has been completed is the standardized test ready to be administered to students for academic credit. While the teacher-made objective test should have a standard way of presenting the directions, test items, and scoring, in practice the test may not be presented the same way for all classes. In the teacher-made objective test, the teacher may read the directions differently or more times on different occasions or in different classes. The teacher may give more examples to one class than another, or the teacher may give more time to one class than to another. On the other hand, this practice should not happen in the standardized objective test. Everything should be done in a standard way.

As noted, there are a number of differences in the teacher-made objective test (the informal test) and the standardized objective test (the formal test). The main differences that always exist between the informal and formal test are in the planning time for the test, the initial testing of the test, the student trials—pilot tests and the national comparison. In the teacher-made, objective test, a teacher may make a test several weeks before giving it, a day before, or even the day that he/she plans to give it. It is seldom thoroughly checked by any one other than the teacher herself or himself for accuracy and fairness or tried out on groups of students before the test is given to students for a grade. The standardized objective test, on the other hand, is supposed to be checked for the accuracy and fairness to students and/or tried out on groups of students before it is given to students for a grade. Unlike the planning and designing time for the teacher-made objective test, which takes a short period of time to prepare, the standardized objective test is tested or validated over a number of years.

COMPARISON OF THE TEACHER-MADE OBJECTIVE TEST AND THE STANDARDIZED OBJECTIVE TEST

TEACHER-MADE OBJECTIVE TEST

The designer or developer of the test knows the students for whom the test is made. The teacher test developer knows what has been taught and what he/she wants the students to master.

The directions, format of the items, and scoring are clear but are not checked by groups of people for accuracy and fairness to the student taking the test.

The construction of the test may be done very quickly, and the test is given to the students without being tested.

STANDARDIZED OBJECTIVE TEST

The designer or developer of the test does not know the specific students for whom the test is made but has general knowledge of students at that age or grade level. The test developer knows what generally should have been taught and mastered in that subject area.

The directions, format of the items, and scoring are clear and have been checked by groups of people for accuracy and fairness to the student group for whom the test is planned.

The construction of the test and preparation take a great deal of time since the directions, test items, and scoring must be checked and revised, if need be, before the test can be given to students for a grade.

When giving the test, the teacher may present the directions differently to one class than another. (He/she may reread directions or give one class more time to take the test than another.)

The directions and scoring are presented in the same way each time the test is given.

The test is not tried out on groups of students throughout America before it is given to students for a grade.

The test is tried out on groups of students throughout America before it is given to students for a grade. (When students take the test for a grade, their scores can be compared to the tryout group or groups.)

There is another difference between the teacher-made objective test and the standardized objective test. This difference is that the teacher-made objective test is an informal test. The standardized objective test is a formal test. In going back to our medical comparison, when a mother places her hand on her child's forehead to determine if he/she has a temperature, this is an informal test. However, if the mother or the doctor uses a thermometer, this would be a formal test. When a mother puts her hand on the forehead of the child, she may correctly or incorrectly say that the child has a temperature. This type of test has been done by mothers for years. However, there is little or no way to check to see that this method is accurate. On the other hand, before the thermometer is ever sold for public use, it has been checked or tested for accuracy. When the thermometer is used correctly by the mother or the doctor, either will get a temperature in numbers that can be compared with the temperature of the child at a later time or with average temperatures of children who are the age of that particular child or with the standard temperature for most human beings.

The main difference between the "hand-on-the-forehead" test and the thermometer test is reliability or consistency and accuracy. With the "hand-on-the-forehead" test, there is no real way to check on the consistency and accuracy; this is an informal test which can give a skilled mother some general information. However, others who do the same test may arrive at different results or opinions. On the other hand, results from the thermometer will be consistent and accurate. The reason for this is that the thermometer has been tested or validated for reliability and accuracy. Validation is the difference between the formal and informal test. In the next chapters, validation as it relates to the achievement test is discussed. It should be noted that the validation process for standardization of tests, as described briefly above, is the same for all tests to be used with large segments of the population.

While the objective test is a relatively new test format within the history of education, the subjective test, which was mentioned at the beginning of this discussion, has been used probably ever since written assessment was used in the school setting. Certainly, it was used in American schools in the eighteenth and nineteenth centuries. Subjective tests are usually essay tests. A quick review will point out the differences between the subjective test and the objective test. In an essay-type/subjective test, the student is presented with a series of questions which should be answered. However, because different students have different points of view on a topic, there may be a number of acceptable answers. The different points of view make subjective tests more difficult to evaluate than the objective test in which there is a single correct answer. The essay format of the subjective test, which requires each student to write out his/her answers, not only makes it more difficult to grade but more time consuming. But it, like the objective test—whether teacher made or standardized—is a part of the school testing history. And, it is invaluable to American school testing past and present.

SUMMARY AND IMPLICATIONS

At the birth of America in 1776, American schools did not represent all in "We the people" nor the "more perfect union" as espoused in the U.S. Constitution. Rather than all children being educated, the children of America's elite were served. The schools were not diverse as "We the people" of the U.S. Constitution envisioned. With the onset of the twentieth century more and more of America's children began to populate America's schools. This increase in the population and the diversity that came with the inclusion of more and more of America's children resulted in many curricular changes, including that of school testing.

In the early school the only testing was teacher made. These tests generally consisted of spelling tests, grammar tests, arithmetic tests, essays, essay tests, and observation. Before the late nineteenth century, the major teacher-made test was the essay or subjective test. The subjective test which usually consisted of a series of questions was fairly easy for the teacher to construct but difficult to grade or evaluate. However, even the test construction was not without problems. As an example, the teacher-made questions of this test may not have included the most important content that was studied. In the area of grading, one difficulty was that the knowledge that the student could produce was combined with his/her point of view of the subject. The teacher's point of view may not have been the same as the student's. Another difficulty was that the form—spelling, grammar, and punctuation—was often graded with the same standard as the content. In other words, it was a matter of producing the correct answer with the correct use of spelling, grammar, and punctuation. Another important fact was that the evaluation of such tests was very time consuming.

In the late nineteenth century the objective test was developed. In contrast to the subjective test, there was a correct or best answer that the student had to select. This selection did not allow for the expression of different points of view or for the grading of the student's form of writing. The ease of scoring made the objective test popular in the populous, diverse schools of the twentieth century. Although the objective test is easy to grade, some teachers challenge its use in tapping critical thinking of students. However, a well-constructed teacher-made test is invaluable in the classroom when used with other forms of evaluation.

Unlike the informal teacher-made tests, the standardized objective test is a formal test. It is a formal test because the test itself has been tested by experts in the subject of the test before it is ever administered or given to a student for a grade. The content is first tested. Then students in the age or grade that the test is intended are assessed to see how consistent the test is. This testing is not for a student grade or for his/her school record. The purpose is to find out whether when the student is given the same test after a time interval, or when the student takes two alternate forms of the test, or when even-odd items on a single test are compared that the student will get the same or similar scores. After this process, but still a part of the testing the test, large groups of students take the test to see how rural, urban, and suburban students do. This test process can take many years and involve numerous students in testing the test. Nationwide tests such as the Stanford Achievement Test, Iowa Test of Basic Skills, California Achievement Test, and others may use many experts and as many as 30,000 students in testing the test.

However, whether considering a formal test like the California Achievement Test or an informal teacher-made test, it is important to remember that any test looks at a sample of student behavior. A test is just a small part of the whole picture of a student's performance.

REFERENCES

Adkins, D. C. (1974). *Test Construction*. Columbus, OH: Charles E. Merrill: A Bell & Howell Company.

Anastasi, A. (1976). *Psychological Testing*. New York: Macmillan.

Barr, R. D. and Parrett, W. H. (1995). *Hope at Last for At-Risk Youth*. Boston: Allyn and Bacon.

Borg, W. R. and Gall, M. (1979). *Educational Research*. New York: Longman.

Farr, R. and Carey, R. (1986). *Reading: What Can Be Measured?* Newark, DE: International Reading Association.

Foner, E. and Garraty, J. A. (Eds.) (1991). *The Reader's Companion to American History.* Boston: Houghton Mifflin.

Ritchie, D. and Broussard, A. S. (1997). *American History: The Early Years to 1877.* Westerville, OH: Glencoe/McGraw-Hill.

Zais, R. S. (1976). *Curriculum Principles and Foundations.* New York: Thomas Y. Crowell. Harper & Row.

CHAPTER TWO

Examining the Birth of the Achievement Tests— Informal and Formal

Performance is knowledge in action.

ROBERT EBEL

Achievement testing is a way of examining student academic performance. It is a way (1) to determine if a student's academic needs are being met, (2) to see if the student is meeting program goals and objectives, (3) to predict a student's future academic success, and (4) to make decisions which improve, support, and enrich the student's performance. The purpose of the school achievement test, then, is to evaluate the student's progress for the above reasons. These achievement tests may be either informal or formal. Testing should provide teachers, students, parents, and the community with some insights into what they must do to nurture, enrich, and improve the learning and growth of each student.

The birth of an achievement test starts with a need. A critical need is to find out information about students that can be used to develop effective learning strategies and approaches for them in general or in the case of students who need special help to design specific approaches and strategies for intervention purposes. Other needs may include the necessity to gain additional information about the progress of the students. As part of the learning continuum, it was necessary at the beginning of the twentieth century to develop assessments which were objective and which would provide a great deal of information about the achievement of students in a short period of time. This need arose because of the increased number and diversity of the student population which the schools began to serve during the last century. There was and still is a need for teachers to gain information on a regular basis about the growth and progress of their students. The results of such ongoing testing allow the teachers, students, and parents to make changes in the approaches, strategies, and materials if they are not meeting the needs of the students. Intervention is employed when it is found that the students are having difficulty attaining the goals and objectives of the program.

The first step in the process of developing an informal teacher-made test or a formal standardized test is to determine what is needed. In the case of the teacher-made test, the teacher may revisit some of his/her past tests over the same material to see how the test could be improved upon or how it could be adapted to a new textbook or revised curriculum. The teacher may also collaborate with teachers in his/her school who teach the same grade or subject or with teachers and others in the field. Students and parents should also be consulted. Additionally, through reading journals and books on testing, the teacher who is developing a test may begin a type of collaboration between himself/herself and those who write on the subject of informal tests and those who write about and/or design formal tests.

This exploration of information is a type of discovery process. The discovery process is utilized by the classroom teacher as he/she gathers information about the students, the materials, the approaches, and best practices in an attempt to improve testing as an avenue to improve learning. Teachers often want to examine concepts that seem exceptionally difficult for students. They scrutinize approaches that appear to be stumbling blocks to the students' learning and those that foster and encourage learning. Similarly, the same inquiry is done by the expert test designer or developer who tries to create a formal standardized test that can be used by large segments of the nation's students and that is academically appropriate. Foremost in this process is the need to find effective and relevant assessments which are aligned with research, contemporary students, and best practices.

Collaboration is needed between those who make the informal assessments and those who make the formal assessments. Teachers can collaborate with the expert or experts by going to workshops and reading books and journals on test development. Experts can collaborate with teachers by visiting classrooms, reading journals where teachers share their needs and successes and by contributing to journals. Both the expert and the teacher can grow by mutual sharing at workshops and seminars on the topic of test development. Both can gain information on testing by listening and sharing concerns, questions, and suggestions as to what is needed and what works in the classroom. Parents, students, and community people may also be consulted. Many voices produce very usable tests whether the tests are formal or informal.

The process of collaboration is very similar to the relationship that occurs between patient and doctor. The doctor talks as well as listens to his/her patient. In the case of very young children the doctor listens to the parent or parents of the children in order to get an informal profile of the patient. A thorough doctor weighs the information and then explains his/her position or suspicions about the medical problem. If the doctor decides to use formal instruments, he/she explains the development of the test, why the test is used, and limitations of the test. Both the doctor and the patient come to understand that numerous types of tests—from the very informal to formal—are needed to get a whole view of a patient. The informal sharing often including probing questions may lead to formal tests such as X-rays, sonograms, ultrasound, or other tests.

Sharing helps the doctor and the teacher to envision better ways to evaluate the problems that they want to eradicate. Sometimes the teacher and/or the doctor feels the need to develop a new test in their respective fields. The reason for the search for the new test may be because the teacher or doctor may find that the information and current informal and/or formal tests to be inadequate. The teacher in the field of education and the doctor in the field of medicine may each feel that more information is needed. The collaboration expands from colleagues to education journals and workshops for the teacher. The doctor follows a similar path in his/her collaboration with colleagues at medical conferences and in his/her reading, writing, and sharing/reporting practical and research findings in medical journals. Such exploration may lead to the determination to design new informal or formal tests.

In fact, the need to secure additional or new test information has been a universal quest of the concerned teacher and doctor. Both the doctor's and the teacher's quests are purposeful. The teacher's motivation is the desire to improve teaching and learning. The doctor's drive is whetted by the desire to improve medical practice, to cure illness and disease, and to improve the quality of life for patients. The teacher's drive is to find ways to develop teaching and learning strategies that will help students learn in meaningful ways and for multiple purposes and for their lifetimes. This exploration is ongoing both in medicine and education. Testing in both fields is just part of the continuum of having a full view of the student or patient. Such ongoing study is needed because conditions in education and in medicine change over time. Miller's (1978) medical book listed the leading causes of death in 1900 to be (1) pneumonia, (2) tuberculosis, (3) diarrhea and enteritis, (4) nephritis, (5) heart disease. Today, the leading causes of death are (1) heart disease, (2) cancer, (3) diabetes, (4) stroke, and (5) accidents. A contrast and comparison of the list for 1900 with the current list would show that heart disease appears on both lists; however, a number of the diseases on the list for 1900 are not usually thought of as life threatening today. If the problems leading to academic school failure of 1900 and today were compared, some of the problems causing such failure would be the same. Some would not. This is because in 1900 only a small percentage of school-age children were in school. Looking back to the late nineteenth century, when only the elite in America were educated, subjective assessments were not a concern. However, with the increase and diversity in school populations beginning in the twentieth century, more objective ways had to be used to evaluate the ever-increasing number of students from many different cultures attending school.

As mentioned above, the major changes in the schools in the twentieth century revolved about the fact that schools began to serve a larger and more diverse population than they had before. The diversity included students who were racially, culturally, socioeconomically, and intellectually diverse. The increasingly diverse school population led to the need for curricular revamping, including testing. In the twentieth century, such changes were needed in an effort to serve segments of the American population that had not been served by the public school in the past. The new population forced schools to explore ways to better serve the changing student body. The exploration resulted in the development of differentiated curriculum and programs to stem the tide of student failure, to increase retention, to accommodate students where English was the second language, to include students with special needs. Such changes in schools undoubtedly bolstered the call for objective ways of measuring the success of the curriculum and learning and for making needed curricular revisions. The necessity to evaluate the success of new efforts became more important with the passage of each decade in the twentieth century since the numbers and diversity of the population compounded. At this time, not only were the successes of the programs on the progress of the students measured, but the effect of the teacher. (Teacher accountability became heavily weighed by student progress.) Currently, more and more school districts are using student test performance as a measure of teacher success. Teacher accountability has given rise to the pervasive use of the relatively new, state-proficiency-type testing. The changing schools affected formal and informal test development.

Many of the changes in informal and formal test development paralleled each other. As mentioned in Chapter one, there are similarities and differences in the test development of these two kinds of tests. One major similarity is the fact that both types of tests usually grow out of the need to investigate information that may not have been examined or tested before or that may have been tested in another way in the past. This section will discuss the beginning steps in the development of the informal and the formal tests. While both types of test grow out of specific needs, the process of development is quite different.

The development of the informal test will be examined first. This is logical since the informal test is the older form of the two. The informal test has always been used in teaching in some form whether the form be oral or written. It has always been an integral part of teaching and learning. It is today and will remain the most used type of test in the future since it is ongoing and fairly easy to develop. Informal assessment is used every day in each classroom in one form or another. It is a teacher's way of measuring how effective teaching and learning in the classroom are or have been.

In fact, it is the informal test of observing and questioning that starts with the child's first teachers—his/her parents and grandparents. You might remember how your own parents and grandparents asked questions after any event which they felt should be a learning experience for you. You, as a parent or caring adult, probably do the same kind of questioning with family children. In a way this helps you evaluate the experience—to point out things that the family child or children should have learned. This is done to hear what the child or children have learned and to correct mistakes or misinterpretations in that learning. Informal observation and questioning continue as the child grows older. As the child nears school age, paper-and-pencil tests may be introduced in the home. The paper-and-pencil test is a forerunner of the teacher-made, paper-and-pencil test that is a common tool in the classroom. Such evaluation is invaluable to the teacher who needs to have many answers about teaching/learning successes and failures and to know on a day-by-day basis how well each student is doing. They also need to know how effective each lesson is, what changes need to be made in teaching, and a myriad of decisions that must be made based on the performance of the child.

Some of the informal tests or assessments are often not even thought of as tests. This is true of informal, oral questioning. However, in the hands of a skilled teacher, oral questioning is just that—a test. Through questioning, the teacher may notice or even record students' responses. Such things as the type of questions which are answered or not answered may give the teacher a great deal of information about the student. Even observation can become a measure of performance when the teacher records what he or she sees and hears. The teacher can compare the observed performance of one child with another, or he/she may compare a specific student's performance on one day with another day. The paper-and-pencil test, though, is what is thought of most often when tests are discussed.

Paper-and-pencil tests—formal and informal—are compared and contrasted in Chapter one. It is the objective teacher-made test that is compared with the formal standardized objective test. Some other informal tests will be presented here. Many of these tests or assessments mentioned are different from the informal objective teacher-made tests compared and contrasted in Chapter one. Two such tests include the informal reading inventory and the informal textbook inventory. Both of these tests grew out of a need that classroom teachers expressed—the need to know how well students could use the assigned class textbook. Further, teachers wanted to know how they could help students to use textbooks better. Many teachers felt that most standardized objective tests did not provide enough information to help them with classroom decision making. Such informal tests as the informal reading inventory or the informal textbook inventory helped teachers to determine how well the students could use their particular class textbook. What are the informal reading inventory and the informal textbook inventory?

As the name informal implies these two assessment tools can be made by the classroom teacher and tailored to meet the needs of specific students in his or her classroom. The first of these assessment tools is the informal reading inventory designed by Ernest Betts in 1946. The purpose of the informal reading inventory is to see if the reading materials are appropriate to a student's reading level. It also helps the teacher determine whether a book or reading material is at a level where the student can read the book on his/her own. This is called the **independent level.** Or, it helps the teacher determine if the book or reading material is at a level where the student can read the book with the aid of the teacher. This is called the **instructional level.** Or, it helps the teacher determine if the book or reading material is too difficult for the student to read even with the aid of the teacher. In this case there may be too many new words and concepts and too many advanced comprehension demands for the student. This is called the **frustration level.** At this level, the teacher needs to use an easier textbook with the student.

The design of the informal reading inventory gives the teacher an opportunity to hear a student's oral reading of short segments of the book. After the oral reading, the student has to answer questions about what he/she has read. Silent reading is done and checked by having the student answer questions about what was read. As a final reading task, the teacher reads aloud to the student. The student has to answer questions about what was read to him/her. This is called the **listening level** or **potential level.** This level refers to the highest level at which a student can listen to material being read to him or her and then answer questions about what was heard. In addition, the vocabulary is checked by having the student read word lists and by responding to the comprehension questions that include vocabulary items. The teacher can follow the format of the informal reading inventory which is found in many books on reading instruction for teachers or tailor the inventory to his/her own needs.

The informal textbook inventory is used to test a student's knowledge of the textbook. Such information as the student's familiarity with the structure of the textbook and its many parts and aids—maps, diagrams, charts, and pictures—is tested. This inventory is like an open-book test since students try to find the answers to the teacher-made questions by exploring the assigned classroom text. The informal textbook inventory is most informative to the teacher and helpful to the students when it is given at the beginning of the school year. The informal textbook inventory was created in 1924 by Alberta Walker and Mary Parkman. Anthony Manzo and Ula Manzo (1990) revisited the creation of Walker and Parkman in their book *Content Area Reading: A Heuristic Approach*.

There are many other informal tests or assessments other than the informal reading inventory and the informal textbook inventory. Among these informal assessments are journals, portfolios, samples of student reading and writing. This category of tests or assessments is usually referred to as **authentic assessments** because it examines the student's skills and knowledge while they are being applied, and it reflects experiences from the real world. In journals, students may record their ideas on a daily basis in a notebook or other form. Looking at such a journal, the teacher, parent, or even the student can see the growth that was made in both skills and knowledge from the beginning to the end of the school year or from grade to grade.

Another such test or assessment is the portfolio. The portfolio may include samples of the student's work which may be arranged by subjects or units. This, like the journal, can show the development of the student's work throughout the year. Both journal and portfolio assessments can be a cumulative record of the student's work for his/her career in school. Samples of the student's reading—recordings—and writing show the same kind of growth and development in knowledge and skills as the journal or portfolio. Further, many authors keep journals. Martin Luther King, Jr., kept a journal. Most artists have portfolios of their work which they show when seeking employment or entering an art show. K S. Goodman, L. M. Bird, and Y. M. Goodman (1991) in *The Whole Language Catalogue: Supplement on Authentic Assessment* speak of authentic tests or assessments as "real ones (tests or assessments) that can and do occur in the real world outside of school."

The informal tests have grown out of a concern of educators and even parents who stress the need to look at tests or assessments that measure growth in actual tools of the classroom. These informal assessments often look at the growth in the process of learning, the "how to" of learning—how to use a book, how to write an essay, how to interpret an algebraic equation. In the case of the informal reading inventory, the student's skills and knowledge are evaluated in terms of the vocabulary and comprehension development needed to read the classroom textbook with meaning. In the case of the informal textbook inventory, the student's understanding and application of the appropriate skills to effectively use the structure and parts of a classroom textbook as well as the aids, such as graphs, diagrams, charts, pictures, and other items are evaluated. Both the informal reading inventory and the informal textbook inventory are important because they look at the student's development in the use of a major tool of learning in school as well as the world away from school. The development and use of these informal assessments were the result of interaction and collaboration with many educators, parents, and researchers who were dissatisfied with current assessments or felt that current assessments did not present a whole picture of the student or students.

Whether a person considers the informal, teacher-made test, the informal reading inventory, the informal textbook inventory, the journal, the portfolio, or reading and writing samples; he/she usually has a model or format to follow. The model for informal assessments may be altered or modified to meet the individual needs of the teacher or the class. In addition, the same teacher may further modify any of the above from class to class.

Whereas the flexibility which is mentioned in the above paragraph may make the teacher-made test especially usable to the designer, who is also the major user, the varied conditions under which the assessment is designed or used can yield different results on different occasions. This can make scoring arbitrary. It also means that it is almost impossible to use the above teacher-made tests to compare students from teacher to teacher, from class to class, from school to school, from district to district, and/or throughout the nation.

The informal tests could be compared to the earlier medical example where the mother informally took her child's temperature by placing her hand on the child's forehead. The child's doctor or nurse would confirm or reject the mother's concerns by using a formal instrument, the thermometer. While informal measures may be helpful, they may not be reliable. In this simple example, the thermometer produces reliable information that can be compared to past and future temperatures of the child and also to what is a normal temperature for children. This points to the need for both the use of informal and formal assessments in medicine as well as education. Not only is there a difference in the reliability of the informal and the formal instrument or test in medicine or in education, there is a difference in the development.

While the development and usually the reliability are different in the informal test when compared to the formal test, fulfilling a test need is certainly as crucial in the formal standardized objective test as it is in the informal test. However, unlike the informal test, the planning, the development, and the testing-of-the-test process of the formal test are very intricate and involved. The reason that the making of the formal test is so much more involved than that of the informal test is primarily because the informal test is prepared for students whom the teacher knows personally. The designer of formal tests, on the other hand, is acquainted with the developmental levels of students for whom the test is designed and is very knowledgeable of the content and skill requirements for that group. While the formal test is prepared for a specific grade level and for specific skill-development levels, the test designer just has a general profile of the students who will take the test. For example, he/she knows what content, materials, and approaches are appropriate and required for third-grade students. The test designer is aware that third-grade students study earth science and other grade or skill-specific information. The formal test is prepared for large segments of the population. The students who take the test may live in Alaska as well as Alabama, California, Connecticut, North Carolina, and North Dakota.

After the considerations for the general population are met, the specific test design and the content are paramount in the mind of the formal test developer. The steps in the process of test development are (1) investigate the need for a new test, (2) identify the age or grade level of the group to be tested by the assessment, (3) solicit definitions of major terms from experts in the field to guide the development if the test covers concepts, approaches, or strategies which are new and/or unique in that content area, (4) determine if the new test will be a group test or an individual test and whether the test will be norm referenced or criterion referenced. After the information for the above items is secured, a plan for the test should be developed.

This plan for an achievement test should include an outline containing the goals and objectives for the test. If it is a general achievement test, it may have parts or subtests. Each subtest may contain items that represent one content area or skill such as mathematics, writing, social studies, or reading. It should also include the cognitive domains or levels of thinking that are tapped. One of the helpful guides as far as cognitive domains or levels of thinking, which has been used in such evaluations, is *Bloom's Taxonomy of Cognitive Domains*. *Bloom's Taxonomy* (1956) outlines levels of thinking: knowledge, comprehension, application, analysis, synthesis, and evaluation. Knowledge refers to the recalling of facts, terms, and basic concepts; comprehension refers to the demonstration of an understanding and use of facts and ideas by doing such things as comparison and contrast; application refers to solving problems by using the knowledge, facts, and rules to solve new problems or construct something; analysis refers to breaking information into parts for examination; synthesis refers to bringing information together in formulating a plan or theory; evaluation refers to making a judgment about information or a concept. Plotting the planned test items on a graph and comparing, restructuring, and revising them to make sure that all cognitive domains or levels of thinking are included in the new test is crucial.

Another important step is to make sure that the items are fair—at the appropriate level as far as content, vocabulary, and sentence construction. A big part of fairness is making sure that the items are without bias or stereotypes. The next step in this test development process is writing and revising the directions and scoring so that they are clear, objective, and reliable for students and teacher-administrators. These standards should be checked again by experts, students, and teachers in the validation phase of test development which will be discussed in Chapter three.

REOCCURRING CONCEPTS

Both formal and informal tests grow out of teaching/learning needs. The chief difference is that the informal teacher-made test usually emerges from individual classroom demands. For the formal test, however, the needs usually develop from a national concern such as the dissatisfaction with the educational progress of large segments of the population. The work of the National Assessment of Educational Progress, which will be discussed later in this book, reflects national concerns.

Collaboration, investigation, and research are the tools of both the designers of informal and formal assessments. These tools in the hands of the designers of informal, teacher-made assessments have a far narrower scope than they do in the hands of designers of formal assessments. In meeting the demands of teachers, investigation has produced such assessments as the informal reading inventory, the informal textbook inventory, the use of classroom journals, classroom portfolios, lab reports, writing and reading across the curriculum, rubrics for evaluating writing, and a multitude of other learning instruments. Many of these informal assessments are also referred to as authentic assessments because they assess learning in a "real-world" way rather than in a school-specific way.

The tools of collaboration, investigation, and research have motivated researchers to develop publications that evaluate formal tests such as Buros' Mental Measurement Yearbook. These tools have forced formal test designers to produce formal tests that are more valid and reliable than they were in the past. These tools have encouraged formal test designers to be meticulous in the development of tests and to think about such important concerns for American children as fairness and the avoidance of bias and stereotypes in formal testing.

While both the formal test and the informal test should be produced with great care and with the learning concerns of the students foremost in mind, it is impossible for the informal teacher-made test to follow as many steps as the formal test does in its developmental stage. This is primarily because neither the time nor the money for a formal test is available to the teacher to develop informal assessments.

There are similarities and differences in the two assessments. Both have advantages and disadvantages and limitations. Both the informal teacher-made test including authentic assessment and the formal test add to the academic picture of a student. They should be used to complement each other.

REFERENCES

Borg, W. R. and Gall, M. D. (1979). *Educational Research*. New York: Longman.

Bloom, B. S. (ed.) (1956). *Taxonomy of Educational Objectives. Handbook I: Cognitive Domain*. New York: David McKay.

Buros, O. K. (1938–2003). *The Mental Measurement Yearbooks*. Highland Park, NJ: Gryphon (1938–1978) Lincoln, NE: University Nebraska Press (1985–2003).

Ebel, R. L. (1980). *Achievement Tests as Measures of Developed Abilities*. In W. B. Schrader (Ed.) *New Directions for Testing and Measurement, No.5, Measuring Achievement and Progress over a Decade: Proceedings of 1979 ETS Invitational Conference*. San Francisco: Jossey-Bass.

Ekwall, E. E. and Shanker, J. L. (1988). *Diagnosis and Remediation of the Disabled Reader*. Boston: Allyn and Bacon.

Goodman, K. (1991). "As I See It. Evaluation in Whole Language: Evaluation in Whole Language." In Goodman, K., Bird, L. B., and Goodman, Y. (eds.) *The Whole Language Catalog*. Santa Rosa , CA: American School Publishers.

Keyser, D. J. and Sweetland, R. (eds.) (1984–2003). *Test Critiques*. Kansas City, MO; Test Corporation of America (1984–1988). Austin, TX: PRO-ED, Inc. (1991–2003).

Manzo, A. V. and Manzo, U. C. (1990). *Content Area Reading: A Heuristic Approach*. Columbus, OH: Merrill.

Miller, B. F. with Galton, L. (1978). *The Complete Medical Guide*. New York: Simon and Schuster.

Smith, C. (ed.) (1990). *Alternative Assessment of Performance in the Language Arts: Proceedings*. Bloomington, Indiana: ERIC Clearinghouse on Reading and Communication Skills and Phi Delta Kappa (Copublished).

CHAPTER THREE

Exploring the Completion of the Formal Achievement Test

The initial accuracy of evaluation and that of later interpretation are of paramount importance to the student, to the family, and to the extended societies in which he will engage.

DOROTHY ADKINS

The final step in the testing of the test—the validation—shows the collaborative nature of the process. It also depicts the great efforts that are taken to ensure (1) that the formal standardized objective test is suitable for the students for whom it is designed, (2) that the test has been evaluated in various ways to be sure that it measures what it states it measures, (According to Akins (1974) "The primary requisite of a test is that it measures what it is desired to measure." (p. 31) According to Anastasi (1976) it is crucial " . . . that the test actually measures what it purports to measure." (p. 28) (3) that the test has been evaluated for consistency, (4) that there have been teachers, experts, and students to evaluate the clarity, objectivity, and reliability of the items, the directions, and scoring during the piloting of the test and other validation processes, (5) that the test has been revised based on the evaluations in the pilot studies, (6) that as part of the testing-of-the-test process, it has been administered to large representative segments of the American population for whom the test is designed, and (7) that tables of the performance of the test group or groups are available for comparison when the new test is ready to be used to secure student scores if the test is a norm-referenced test. The final steps all occur before the test is ever given to students as a formal assessment for their school or home records.

FORMAL TEST VALIDATION

One important collaboration in the validation process is with the students for whom the test is intended. In modern times, there are a number of expressions that state how much our students are valued. One of these statements is that, "Students are our most important resource." This statement is really true in the validation process. Students play a major role in formal test development in pilot studies where their input is solicited and used. The importance of students' thoughts is eloquently expressed by Kahlil Gibran (1966) in the *Prophet*. Gibran gives this admonition to parents about their children which is also very appropriate for teachers and test designers:

> *You may give them your love but not your thoughts,*
> *For they have their own thoughts.*
> *You may house their bodies but not their souls,*
> *For their souls dwell in the house of tomorrow, which you cannot visit,*
> *not even in your dreams.*
> *You may strive to be like them, but seek*
> *not to make them like you.*
> *For life goes not backward nor tarries with yesterday. . . .*

For this reason children or students should be our collaborators. Their thoughts and perceptions are different from adults—from parents, teachers, and test designers. This is a critical part of the development of the formal test. However, in the preparation of the informal teacher-made tests, it is only the stellar teacher who solicits the thoughts or ideas of students when he/she prepares a test for use in his/her classroom. It would be wise if students' thoughts were part of the thinking and planning process of the teacher-made test. Some very insightful teachers do consult students even in constructing an informal assessment.

In the testing of the formal test, students' (children's) thoughts are valued. The students themselves can provide the prospective of the group the test is designed for. In testing the test, the test designers have remembered the warning of Gibran that the children's thoughts and understanding are different from that of adults. Students' voices are heard. As part of the development and validation of the formal test, small groups of students take the test and have the test scored. Scoring at this stage, however, is not to have the test results placed on students' records but rather to test the test. This stage of test development and validation is called the piloting of the test. After the students take the test as part of the piloting stage, they are asked questions about the clarity, fairness, and suitability of the test items in general and specifically about the items that each student missed. After hearing the students' answers about the test items or questions, items are revised to make them clearer, fairer, and more suitable to the student population that will be taking the test. Questions are also asked of the students about the clarity, fairness, and suitability of the directions and scoring. Directions and scoring are revised based on the input of the students in the pilot study. This collaboration with students is an invaluable part of the validation of the test.

If you recall the steps that were taken at the beginning of this test development and validation processes, you will note that the process is truly collaborative. The collaborative nature is seen in the number of people who should be consulted and the research that should be done in the process of developing and validating the test. Books, experts, teachers (practitioners), parents, and students should be consulted. Experts should be asked to define the tested concept if it is new or unique in the area of testing. Initially, experts should be asked to complete questionnaires about the possibility of developing such a test.

LEVELS OF THINKING

Not only does the use of students show the collaborative nature of the validation process, but it shows the thoroughness of the process since it requires the students to examine and evaluate the test. One of the things that students cannot do in their evaluation is judge the level of thinking required for the test items. It is the test designer or expert who has to do this. It is wise for the test designer to revisit the construction of test items and evaluate them to determine the level of thinking required for each item. Such checking will assure that questions represent items that evaluate different levels of thinking or cognitive domains. This is an important step since a good test taps various levels of thinking.

As an example, a question on a history test that asks the student to identify the first president of the United States is just asking the student to recall something that could be easily learned by looking in an encyclopedia or history book or on the Internet. This is the knowledge domain or thinking level. Questions should be asked that require the student to organize, compare/contrast, translate, and/or interpret information. This is the comprehension level. Questions or items should be included in the test that require the student to apply facts, knowledge, and rules in new or different ways to solve a problem.

This is the application level. Other questions or items that should be included are those that require the student to break information into parts. This is analysis. Having questions that require students to put information together to arrive at an answer would be tapping the synthesis level. Questions should be provided that require the student to judge information. This is called evaluation. Whereas a number of the tasks that are done in formal test development cannot be done in informal test development because of the time and money they require, checking a test to see that the items tap the various levels of thinking or cognitive domains can and should be done for informal as well as formal tests.

VALIDITY

Another collaborative process seen in the evaluation of the test is the securing of validity. As part of the validation process, experts check the content of the test for accuracy and suitability for the grade level of the students for whom the test is designed. Or, textbooks on that subject for the grade-level students for whom the test is intended can be consulted to determine whether the test items or questions correlate with the content of the books. For example, the designer of a new formal mathematics test for fourth-grade students could compare the items or questions on his/her test with fourth-grade mathematics textbooks that are used in a wide range of fourth-grade classrooms nationally. The validity is checked to see if a test measures what the test designer says it measures.

The steps which are briefly described in the above paragraph represent the process for evaluating content validity. The two ways for evaluating content validity are cited above—having experts in the content area or subject of the test evaluate the test or comparing the test with the content of textbooks on the subject at the grade level of students for whom the test is designed. While there are other forms of validity which will be briefly described in this chapter, evaluating the content validity of any test is crucial. It, therefore, should always be part of the validation process. (For both validity and reliability, which will also be discussed in this chapter, statistical formulas are used. However, these formulas are beyond the scope of this book.)

One of the things that the experts would look for in a new test is whether the items in the test are appropriate for the grade level of the test. If the items are not appropriate, not only would the test lack content validity, but it would be unfair for the students who would take it. If the test designer states that the test is a third-grade mathematics test, the test should be checked by experts to see if they agree that the test actually measures third-grade level mathematics. As a new teacher or parent, you might wonder how a third-grade mathematics test would not measure third-grade mathematics. One way is that the items or questions may not be appropriate for third graders. The items or questions may actually be on the second-grade level, and therefore, too easy for third-grade students. Or, the items may really be at the fourth-grade level, and, therefore, be unfair because they represent items that have not yet been taught. The average third-grade student will be unable to complete the problems.

Another problem that the expert examining the new test for content validity might find is that while the test is said to measure mathematics, it does not. The expert may find that the test designer has included an excessive amount of reading on the test. The test designer may have included all or nearly all story problems in an attempt to make the test very challenging. However, rather than evaluating the student's mathematics skills, the excessive inclusion of story problems may in reality be measuring the student's reading skills. Having the items checked initially by an expert in the field of third-grade mathematics or checked by the test designer by reviewing or consulting numerous third-grade mathematics books which are used nationally is part of the validation process to assure that the test has content validity.

As might be imagined, there are different types of validity. Content validity of a new test, as stated above, is determined in two ways, and in both cases such examinations would produce percentages of agreement. One percentage of agreement is among the subject experts based on their assessment of the subject and grade-level appropriateness of the test items. The second would be the agreement of the test items with numerous textbooks on the same content and grade level—similarity of skills and concepts. (The examination of the books would be conducted by the test designer or by the researchers.) As an example, if most third-grade mathematics textbooks included addition, subtraction, fractions, story problems, graphs, and charts as part of content to be learned and the problems to be solved, a mathematics test for third-grade students would have a high percentage of agreement of the content if these concepts and skills were included on the new test. Again, this is content validity.

Another validity which should be determined for each test is face validity. This validity includes such features of the new test as the format, style, and appearance—basically how the test looks. Does the test look like one developed for the designated grade level of the test? For example, a test for the second-grade level may have clowns or "happy faces" or other objects from the school or home experiences of a second grader may be incorporated into the questions. Tests developed for eleventh or twelfth- grade students would be devoid of pictures except figures or objects that are subject specific such as an octagon or a microscope. While this may not seem to be essential, it is important that the test look like a test and that the examples be appropriate for the students. While face validity is important, many researchers caution teachers and other educators about using face validity as the sole standard for selecting a formal standardized objective test.

In each of the validities below, the newly developed test is correlated or checked to see the degree of relationship that exists with another test or event. Below **criterion-related validity, concurrent validity**, and **predictive validity** are described. These are three other commonly used validities. **Construct validity** is also a commonly used validity and is only briefly described here because it is used to determine the correlation of tests that examine such psychological concepts as intelligence and aptitude.

Criterion-related validity correlates a person or student's on-the-job experience with the student's performance on a test. As an example, if the topic of a new test is reading, it should correlate highly with the task of reading. Put another way, if the child can read and understand his/her grade-level book and summarize or retell or correctly answer critical questions about the book, he/she should be able to pass the reading portion of a grade-level-appropriate achievement test. Comparing the student's actual reading performance with such a student's test performance should show very similar performance. This correlation of or comparison between the actual performance, the criterion, and the test performance produces criterion-related validity.

Concurrent validity can be computed when the student's scores on the new test are compared with an existing established test. If the new test is an achievement test of subjects such as reading, writing, social studies, and science on the student's grade level, his/her results on the new test could be compared or correlated with the student's performance on a long-standing test like the California Achievement Test, which assesses achievement in the same subject areas. If the student had a score that identified him/her as "advanced" on the California Achievement Test, he/she should also be classified similarly on the new test. The student's test results on the new test and the long-standing test should be very similar. The idea behind this validity is that if the new test measures the same subject areas as an existing test, the results can be compared or correlated. To look at an even more practical example: as an adult if you are an experienced, safe driver in an old car that is in good running condition, under similar circumstances, you should be a safe driver in a similar new car. Few people who are experienced, safe drivers become poor drivers when they purchase a new car which is similar to the former car and driven under the same or similar conditions. On the other hand, a poor driver in a well-running, safe old car will under the same conditions perform poorly in a new car. In concurrent validity, the student's performance on a newly developed test is correlated with the student's performance or the results of his/her performance on an existing long-standing test.

In predictive validity, two pieces of information are compared. The test results would be one piece of information. The student's future performance in an area, either success or failure, could be the second piece of information. The performance usually occurs a year or more after the test. For example, reading readiness tests are used to predict a preschooler's later reading performance. The popular American College Test (ACT) and the Scholastic Aptitude Test (SAT) are used to predict a student's future college or academic success. A newly developed test could be used to see how well it predicts some future performance. The better it predicts some future performance, the more valid the test would be.

Most textbooks on tests and measurement include construct validity in a discussion of validity. A construct is related to psychological concepts such as intelligence, creativity, or aptitude. A test designer may think and research may imply that an intelligent person is also creative. A test designer of a new intelligence test may compare the performance of student participants in the validation of his/her test with an existing test on creativity. The results of the comparison would be a measure of construct validity. (A textbook on tests and measurement should be consulted if you wish to explore this type of validity.)

RELIABILITY

Checking the test for consistency is another critical part of the validation process—the testing of the test. As a review, validation includes evaluating a new test for validity and reliability. Generally, validity means that a test measures what it states it measures. As stated in a previous example, the test designated as a third-grade mathematics test must measure third-grade mathematics in order to be valid. The other part of the validation process is reliability. Reliability has to do with the degree of consistency that a new test has with itself in various ways. Reliability is tested when two test scores for each student in the test group are compared. The two scores for each participant are found by having the same test administered to the students in the test group twice, by having the students take two different forms of the same test, or by dividing the student's single test performance into two parts and then comparing the parts. The reason for this comparison is that the same person taking the new test on separate occasions should get two scores that are the same, nearly the same, or similar. While a test will not be as exacting as the thermometer in our previous example, if it is reliable, it should provide the same or very similar results when given under the same conditions on different occasions.

These scores are then compared. There are three methods of measuring reliability. In one method, the test could be given twice to each person in the test group. It could be administered to the test-group students at a designated time and re-administered to the same students a second time about two weeks later. The results from the two administrations could be compared or correlated. This is method is called **test-retest reliability.**

A second method is to use two different forms of the new test; for instance, Form A and Form B. Both forms are taken by each student test participant. The two scores are then compared. This method is called **alternate or equivalent form reliability.** In the third method, the test could be given once. The single test could be divided or split into two parts. One part could consist of all the even-numbered items. The second part could consist of all of the odd-numbered items. A score would be determined for each part. The performance of each student in the test group on the two parts would be compared. This method is called **split-half reliability.** Each student has two scores. The two scores are compared. There is another method of determining reliability which shows how consistent each item is with the entire test. Like split-half reliability, in this method only one administration of the test is done, and each item is compared to the entire test. The more alike the task of each item is with the task of the entire test the greater the consistency. This method determines **inter-item consistency**.

In the reliability methods above, the two scores from a single student are compared. The comparison is called correlation. Correlation is the degree of relationship that one thing has with another thing. A correlation can be positive or negative. An example of a positive correlation is found when the test scores of a student are compared with some other performance of a student such as grade point average. If both performances are high, this would be a high positive correlation or comparison. A negative correlation or comparison would be one where a student who earns a high score on a test has low grades or grade point average. In predictive validity, two pieces of information from a single student are compared. The test results would be one piece of information. The student's future performance in reading or success or failure in college could be the second piece of information. The performance usually occurs a year or two after the test. Such is the case in the use of reading readiness test scores. Correlation also occurs in the reliability process. For example in test-retest reliability, the student's score on the first administration of the test is compared with the student's score on the second administration of the test that is taken after a time interval of about two weeks.

In the above methods, there are two scores for one student. If the two scores for this student are just the same, there would be 100% or 1.00 agreement or correlation. In the case of the thermometer, the average or normal temperature when taken on two occasions under the same conditions would be 98.6° on each occasion. This would be a perfect positive correlation. Seldom would the two test scores, using any of the reliability or validity methods mentioned above, be just the same. If the test designer has developed a test that is reliable, the two scores from the above processes would be similar. This is true for the validation processes when test scores are compared. The closer that the scores are to 100% or 1.00, the higher the relationship or correlation. If a student test-study participant received a score of 90 on one test and a score of 92 on the second test, the performance of the student on both test would be very consistent. The reliability or validity would be very high. On the other hand, if the score of the student on the first test was 10 and the score on the second test was 79, the scores would not be consistent, and the reliability would be low. In checking the reliability for a new test when correlated with itself or with another form of the new test, the results of the correlation should be very high from the 80% or .80 to the 99% or .99 range. The comparison of the two scores on each student on the new test would be examined. If two hundred students were used to determine reliability of a test, there would be two hundred correlations. (There are formulas for computing reliability and validity correlations that can be found in a textbook such as Borish's 2003 *Educational Testing and Measurement.*)

When both reliability and validity have been determined for the new test, the test is said to be validated. As a review, validity involves checking a test to determine whether it measures what it states it measures. Reliability involves checking the consistency with which the test measures the subject of the test.

NORMING GROUP

In addition to the above—involved and time-consuming processes in validating the formal standardized test—the process is only finished when the completed test has been tried out nationally on a large, diverse group of students who represent a sample of the American school population and the intended grade level of the new test. For the norm-referenced test, the scores of this group, known as the norming group, are placed in tables so that test administrators can compare the scores and ranks of future test takers with the norming group. This also is a time-consuming undertaking. Many students and test administrators are involved. As an example, a revision of the California Achievement Test used 30,000 students to participate in the norming. It is crucial that the norming or normative group of students should represent the broad, national spectrum of students at the age or grade level of the test in order for the use of the norms tables be valid.

STANDARD ERROR OF MEASUREMENT

When the validation process is complete, there are other considerations that must be weighed. One is that even an excellent standardized formal test is not perfect. There are errors in all measurement. This is called the standard error of measurement. This concept relates to the fact that any test score is made of two parts. One part represents the actual task that is being tested or measured. This is known as true score. The other part represents errors in measurement. The lower the reliability correlation, such as .40, the more errors in the test. The low reliability correlation of .40 means that only 40 percent of the score represents true score, and 60 percent represents errors in the test or measure. The closer the reliability correlation is to 1.00, such as .90, the fewer errors in the measurement. To incorporate the concepts of true score and errors in measurement, statisticians stress that any score be examined in a range or band rather than the achieved score or points—the raw score. The formula for computing true score uses the reliability correlation and the variance of the group test scores to calculate the standard error of measurement. This formula determines the range within which a true score would be found. As a hypothetical example, consider a test which was found to have a reliability correlation of .40 in the validation process. On this test, a student achieves a score of 75. The computation shows that the band in which the true score is found is ±15 of the achieved score. The calculation (75–15 and 75+15) would show that the true score could be as low as 60 or as high as 90. The same score of 75 when the reliability correlation for the test was .90 may be in a range or band that is ±4 of the achieved score, so that the true score may be as low as 71 or as high as 79. (There is a formula for computing the standard error of measurement. You will find it in a book on tests and measurement such as Kubizyn and Borish's (2003) *Testing and Measurement*, mentioned above, or Adkins' (1974) *Test Construction*.) It cannot be stressed too often how important it is to remember that there are errors and limitations to all tests and research.

Another critical issue was raised by Oscar Buros as long ago as 1938 that even though a number of tests may claim to be standardized and validated, the truth is that some may not have been evaluated for reliability or validity. Others may only have face validity—they look like tests. Because of his negative experiences with formal tests, Buros (1938) developed the *Mental Measurement Yearbook*. The *Mental Measurement Yearbook* consists of many large volumes, where experts in testing evaluate new tests and revisions of tests. In 1984, a second series of volumes *Test Critiques* was developed which evaluates new tests or revisions of tests. (Keyser and Sweetland, 1984)

CRITICAL CONCEPTS AND IMPLICATIONS

The completion of the validation process—finding validity and reliability—separates the formal test from the informal test. The validation process is very thorough and time consuming. In assessing the validity to determine that a test measures what it says that it measures, the following types of validity may be computed: content, criterion-related, construct, concurrent, or predictive. Face validity can be determined by inspecting the test. Reliability is the consistency of the test results when the test is compared with itself or another form of the new test. Reliability can be computed by comparing two scores or results of the test in one of the following ways: test retest, alternate or equivalent form, or split half.

Even with the proposed thoroughness of the validation process, there are considerations which should be foremost in the mind of teachers and educators as they plan to use any assessment. These considerations are that no matter how excellent a test is reported to be, no test is perfect. There is an error in all measurement, the standard error of measurement, and there are limitations to all tests.

The Mental Measurement Yearbook and *Test Critiques* were both developed so that experts in the field of testing and measurement can evaluate, critique, and write about the reliability and validity of new tests and revisions of tests. And, educators, researchers, and parents can use this information as a reference.

Validation of formal tests is crucial since such tests are intended to be used with large segments of the population. Hopefully, even an informal teacher-made test should be valid and reliable; however, only the formal test goes through the validation or the testing-of-the-test process.

In *Test Construction*, Adkins (1974) discusses true score which stems from the validation process. She states that low test scores may stigmatize and discourage students. She acknowledges this but says, "Some truth lies in this claim, in part attributable to improper use of test scores by people who fail to realize that scores do not signify points but rather, with certain assumptions ranges within which true scores . . . lie at a specifiable level of confidence."

REFERENCES

Adkins, D. C. *(1974)*. *Test Construction*. Columbus. OH: Charles E. Merrill: A Bell & Howell Company.

Anastasi, A (1976). *Psychological Testing*. New York: Macmillan.

Berk. R. A. (ed.) (1986). *Performance Assessment Methods and Applications*. Baltimore: Johns Hopkins University Press.

Bloom, B. S. (1971). *Handbook on Formative and Summative Evaluation on Student Learning*. New York: McGraw–Hill.

Borg, W. R. and Gall, M. D. (1979). *Educational Research: An Introduction*. New York: Longman.

Buros, O. K. (1938–2003). *The Mental Measurement Yearbooks*. Highland Park, NJ: Gryphon (1938–1978) Lincoln, NE: University Nebraska Press (1985–2003).

Cangelosi, J. S. (1990). *Designing Tests for Evaluating Student Achievement*. New York: Longman.

Chase, C. I. (1974). *Measurement for Educational Evaluation*. Reading, MA: Addison-Wesley.

Ebel, R. L. (1980). "Achievement Tests as Measures of Developed Abilities." In W. B. Schrader (ed.) *New Directions for Testing and Measure No. 5, Measuring Achievement and Progress over a Decade: Proceedings of 1979 ETS Invitational Conference*. San Francisco: Jossey-Bass.

Gellman, E. S. (l995). *School Testing: What Parents and Educators Need to Know*. Westport, CO: Prager.

Gibran, Kahlil, (1966). *The Prophet*. New York: Knopf.

Keyser, D. J. and Sweetland, R. (eds.) (1984–2003). *Test Critiques*. Kansas City, MO: Test Corporation of America 1984–1988). Austin, TX: PRO-ED (1991–2003).

Kubizyn, T. and Borish, G. (2003). *Educational Testing and Measurement*. New York: Wiley

Lipson, M. Y. and Wixson, K. K. (1997). *An Assessment and Instruction of Reading and Writing Disability, An Interactive Approach*. New York: Longman.

Popham, W. J. (1995). *Classroom Assessment: What Teachers Need to Know*. Boston: Allyn and Bacon.

Rothman, R. (1995). *Measuring Up: Standards, Assessment, and School Reform*. San Francisco: Jossey-Bass.

CHAPTER FOUR

Peering Through the Kaleidoscope of Tests and Their Uses and Results

> Clearly one of the new technologies that must be put in place is a means of measuring the qualitative aspects of schoolwork for it is by such qualitative results that schools of the future must lead.
>
> PHILLIP A. SCHLECHTY

Schlechty's (1990) quotation above from *Schools For the Twenty-first Century* and current practices do indeed represent a kaleidoscope as far as formal and informal achievement assessments used in the schools. The evaluation pendulum is swinging. The test kaleidoscope is moving to another phase.

In Chapter one, the fact that there was almost exclusive use of the teacher-made, subjective qualitative test in the nineteenth-century schools was discussed. In the twentieth century, however, the special assessment needs caused by the increase both in school diversity and population and the dissemination of the objective test nudged educational institutions closer and closer to wide usage of the objective, quantitative test. The quantitative tests gave the results in numbers—for example, 1600 on the Scholastic Aptitude Test (SAT) or scores at the 96th percentile. By the end of the twentieth century and the beginning of the twenty-first century, knowledge/learning was/is often equated with a number. This is quite different from the nineteenth-century essay examinations or essays, which were rated by the quality of the answer or essay as poor, fair, good, excellent.

The purpose of this chapter is to present a brief discussion of the major types of formal achievement tests. This grows out of the discussion of the way formal tests are developed and validated in Chapter three. The rationale for the use of formal tests as well as some of their limitations will be presented. Informal teacher-made tests and other informal teacher-made tools will also be discussed. Additionally, it will be shown how the pendulum is still swinging with the current effort to quantify essays and essay-type answers by including check-lists, rubrics, and other things which make essays less subjective and less qualitative. Also, the value of Schlechty' s thought when he states that an important responsibility of school of the future is "measuring the qualitative aspects of schoolwork . . ." will be weighed. Finally, there will be a brief discussion of quantitative scores for formal assessments and qualitative scores for many informal tests.

Before discussing the formal objective test, it is important to present the reason why formal objective tests currently play such an important role in contemporary schools. As mentioned throughout this book, the twentieth century saw an influx of students into America's schools. There were not only more students than ever before, but the students were more diverse. At the same time, the explosion of the mass media, including the radio, television, movies, and others dissolved some of the past isolation that had existed from educational community to educational community. There was a need to know how local schools—rural, urban, and suburban—compared with the schools nationally. In order to make comparisons, tests have to be valid, reliable, objective, fair, suitable, comparable, and economical in time as well as in money. The formal objective standardized test seemed to fit this bill. The formal achievement tests that will be presented are norm-referenced and criterion-referenced.

Both formal norm-referenced tests and criterion-referenced tests have been validated—evaluated for validity and reliability. As discussed in Chapter three, in the final step of the validation process, large groups of students nationally from the grade level for which the new test was intended take the test. In the norm-referenced test, the norm group is used as a standard by which the local schools can determine whether the students in their district are functioning above, at, or below the national norm group. The standards set by the norming group become the norm—the yardstick for the evaluation of student performance. (There are also local norms that allow the class, school, or school district to know how their students compare to other students in their class, school, or district.) Formal criterion-referenced tests have a predetermined standard, usually the attainment of a required number of points—the criterion—which students must achieve in order to pass. In the case of a criterion-referenced test to be used nationally, the criterion or standard should be based on national objectives and goals for students at the grade level of the test.

NORM-REFERENCED TESTS

Norm-referenced formal objective tests are the most common of the standardized tests. Even the intelligence test, like the achievement test, is a norm-referenced test. In the norm-referenced test, the local students' test results on formal tests are compared to the performance of the national norm group who are the same age or grade-level as the students taking the test. Some commonly used group achievement tests are the California Achievement Test, Comprehensive Test of Basic Skills, Iowa Test of Basic Skills, Iowa Test of Educational Development, Metropolitan Achievement Tests, and Stanford Achievement Test. Some of the achievement tests like the Wechsler Individual Achievement Test are designed to be given individually. Most survey tests, which measure general achievement, are often norm referenced. Diagnostic tests, which are used for intervention programs to find the areas of student weakness in a particular skill area, are norm-referenced tests and may be administered to the group or individual.

CRITERION-REFERENCED TESTS

Criterion-referenced tests, as mentioned above, are tests where the individual's test results are measured against a predetermined standard. This standard is usually based on national goals and objectives for that grade level. Some of the most commonly used criterion-referenced tests are the state proficiency tests which are common to most states in the United States. On the proficiency tests, there are predetermined standards that a student must achieve in a subject or subtest in order to pass. The subtests are usually designed to test reading, writing, social studies, mathematics, and science. This predetermined standard is based on the quantity of material or learning that represents the level that is thought to show competency. The mastery test is another form of criterion-referenced test. It is often used to see which achievement skills have been mastered and which skills need to be reviewed, reinforced, and then retested.

INFORMAL ASSESSMENT

Informal Assessments can be thought of as tests or various types of assessments which have not been tested for reliability and validity. Informal tests have been part of evaluation in education long before the advent of formal assessment and are used with greater frequency than formal assessment. These assessments come in various forms. In the late twentieth century and early twenty-first century, many informal assessments have come to be called authentic assessments namely because such assessments measure growth and progress on "real, everyday materials" or in "real, everyday ways." Further, these informal or authentic assessments evaluate skill development in an ongoing way.

This use of informal assessments has come about because many educators have found that the formal objective tests do not provide them with the practical knowledge necessary to address their students' learning needs. Also, many teachers and other educators feel that a lot of the current formal tests do not reflect the findings of research.

A few of the informal assessments will be briefly described here. All teacher-made materials that are created to assess student behavior could be called informal tests or assessments. The informal objective test, which has been discussed earlier, is a familiar item in almost every classroom. A less common but very effective tool is the informal textbook inventory that is designed to evaluate a student's ability to use all parts of a textbook. It can be used as a mastery-type test because the teacher can provide students with review, reinforcement, and retesting on parts of the book that the students do not know. For example, if the results of an informal textbook inventory showed that the student or students could not extract information from diagrams, graphs, maps, or charts, these items could be built into everyday learning experiences in the classroom.

In a similar category is the informal reading inventory that is used to measure the "goodness of fit of a book." The recommended procedure for administering the informal reading inventory is to test reading in the textbook in a number of ways: (1) to test passages from the beginning, middle, and end of the book; (2) to have the student read aloud and then check his/her comprehension on the passage; (3) to have the student read silently and then check his/her comprehension on the passage; (4) to have the student listen to a passage read by the teacher and then answer comprehension questions based on the passage. (This process is called evaluating the listening level, which is also called the capacity or potential level of the student.) The student's knowledge of vocabulary is also assessed. Further, the student's ability to unlock unfamiliar words can be observed during his/her oral reading. Using this inventory, the teacher can determine whether the class textbook is too easy for the student; this would be the independent level. A book at the level where the student can use it with some assistance from the teacher is at the instructional level and represents the right level for classroom instruction. Or, the book could be at the frustration level for the student. At this level, there are too many unknown words and concepts for the student to read the book even with the aid of the teacher. The informal reading inventory could also be used as a group assessment. There are also commercially-developed informal reading inventories.

Another informal assessment is the **cloze test**. The classroom teacher can adapt this test to meet the specific needs of his/her classroom; however, the standard cloze test is based on a 250-word passage. The first and last sentences are left intact. Then, in the other sentences every fifth word is deleted. In place of the deleted words should be blanks that are uniform in length. The students are asked to fill in the blank with the word that has been deleted. However, if the student misspells the deleted word, he/she is not penalized for the misspelling.

In addition to the informal use of such tests as informal textbook inventories, informal reading inventories, and the cloze test, there are a number of informal assessments that could also be categorized as authentic assessments because they represent items that the professional uses. In the case of classroom assessments, many of the tests are school specific—they will only be found in the school classroom. An example is the true-false test. This same specific-to-the-classroom quality is not found in authentic assessment, which could include such things as journals, lab reports, essays, essay answers, portfolios, photographic essays, and others. These are the *real materials* of the professional.

Writers often record day-to-day routine occurrences or special events in a journal. Artists display their work in portfolios. Scientists record their notes and findings as lab reports. Probably included in this category are writings where students create products. These include student-written books, school newspapers, science projects, and inventions that are real-world products. In addition, these products are evaluated in much the same way as when they are produced by the professional, that is, through holistic assessment. Holistic assessment, where an evaluator may assess a product as a whole and make general suggestions, is often used in authentic assessment. A teacher/evaluator with such products as books, newspapers, science projects, and inventions will use the same type of assessment as an editor does with a reporter or an author. The editor may tell the reporter to include more specific adjectives. The editor may tell the author to change the ending of a book or even to delete material to reduce the length of the book. Many schools have adopted these and other forms of informal or authentic assessments to their repertoire of testing.

The weighing of Schlechty's statement, found at the beginning of this chapter, might be appropriate here before looking at changes in informal instruments. Schlechty emphasizes the crucial importance that schools in the twenty-first century focus on the qualitative aspect of students' work. His thought is true to a large extent. However, it seems to just focus on the finished product—the expected outcome. Certainly in exposing students to authentic assessments, it is the outcome that is valued—the excellent book; the efficient, new product; the life-saving invention. So, as a person looks at the results, it is the qualitative aspect of any item or product that is valued. But Schlechty's thought reflects an idea that he may have forgotten, and that is that behind every quality product or almost every quality product is a quantitative aspect.

Seldom is the quantitative product displayed in any way in the finished product. In the medical field, the doctor-prescribed medicine does not list all the steps in the process of making and testing the drug nor the milligrams of each drug included in the process—the quantitative process. (There may be statements included with the drug that warn of possible side effects.) Both the doctor and the patient are concerned about the qualitative part, about whether the drug will relieve pain and/or cure illness. Similarly, it is only the tailor who is concerned about how much fabric is needed to make a man or woman's suit. He/she is concerned with how the pattern must be placed on the fabric in preparation for cutting out the suit. The tailor determines whether a seam will be one-half or three-fourths inch or whether a hem will be one or two inches. These quantitative parts are crucial if a well-fitting, stylish garment is to be produced. But the consumer is concerned about the fit, the style, the finish—the qualitative aspects.

In education and other institutions, the quantitative aspects are often heavily valued when there are no qualitative aspects to examine. Recently, I saw the following saying on a Hallmark fresh/ink card. On the outside it read, "Rude Awakening #457." On the inside it read, "Nobody really cares what your GPA was." This, like Schlechty's (1990) statement, is true to some degree. It is untrue, however, for the new college graduate student who has no quality products except a professional-looking resume, which may or may not have been self produced. Without the qualitative aspects, the quantitative GPA of the new college graduate may speak volumes to the new employer.

These scenarios and the critique of Schlechty's statement suggest that there is a marriage between quantitative and qualitative experiences and assessments, like essays and essay answers. Many teachers and other educators often provide students with checklists, analytic scoring sheets, rubrics, or holistic scoring when students are asked to write an essay or essay answers. A checklist can be used in two ways. One way could be to provide the student with a checklist that he or she should use to guide an essay or essay answers. Another way is for the teacher to use a checklist of the writing process as part of the evaluation of the essay or essay answers. On the second type of checklist, the teacher lists the steps in the writing process and notes the steps that should be included in an essay. The teacher checks off the steps that are included, and this helps to determine the student's grade. In the analytic scoring sheet, the teacher or evaluator determines a possible number of points for an essay; the points are then divided into categories such as **content, structure, mechanics,** and others. Under each of these categories specific requirements are noted. The student receives points based on the number of requirements that he/she has included in the essay or essay answers.

Another approach is the use of a rubric to list the characteristics of the different levels of writing and the point value of each level. For example, a **4** might be given for an essay that has all the desired characteristics; a **3** for an essay that contains most of the desired characteristics; a **2** for an essay that contains some of the desired characteristics; a **1** for the essay that contains only a few of the desired characteristics; and a **0** might be given for an essay that is unscorable.

Included in other types of scoring is holistic scoring which can be used for evaluating the essay for specific things—the use of complete sentences, the use of vivid adjectives. Or, holistic scoring could be used for evaluating the essay as a whole. In this evaluation the teacher often has outstanding essays of other students at the same grade level to use as a standard to measure the other papers. The student papers that are used for comparing and grading the other student papers are called **anchors or benchmarks.** The grading strategies that are used above are ways to make the subjective, qualitative aspect of writing more objective and more quantifiable. The use of these strategies shows the marriage between what once was a very subjective, qualitative process to one that incorporates the quantitative process to make essay evaluation fairer and more objective than it has been in the past.

Even the quantitative test scores are often tempered with a qualitative aspect. This concept will be revisited as the results from formal objective tests are discussed. The two types of formal objective achievement tests which usually produce quantitative results are the norm-referenced test and the criterion-referenced test. As we know, the norm-referenced test has that name because the results of students are compared with other students at the same age or grade level who were part of the norming group. After the specific score is received for each student, the student's score is changed statistically and then compared with lists of students nationally who were part of the norming group. The categories of scores are generally below average, average, above average. These scores could be plotted on the normal curve. (The normal curve is an imaginary curve where the greatest number of people would be clustered in the middle of the curve and would form a shape like a bell and represent the average group. On the left side of the bell-shaped curve, also referred to as the normal curve, would be found the scores of students who performed below average on the specific test. On the right side of the bell-shaped curve are the scores of students who performed above average on the specific test. The normal curve is used to compare various behaviors, traits, or attributes such as a person's performance on a test or even his/her height or weight.) The range of scores from below average to above average can be represented in different ways. Below, the following are some of the varied ways that scores are shown on the normal curve: percentile scores, stanines, intelligence scores, and grade equivalent scores. There are other ways that scores can be used to describe the relationship of an individual's score with the group, but only these four will be shown here.

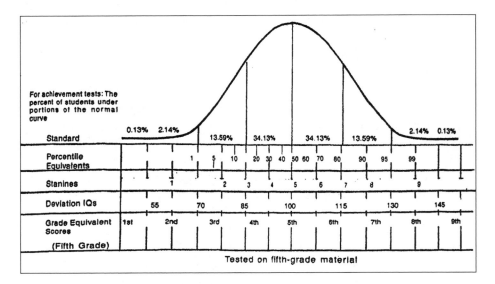

The information presented above shows different ways that scores may be compared. In each case, the reporting of the scores places a student in categories that show his/her test performance as below average, average, or above average. The percentile score or percentile rank shows the percent of students nationally who scored below that rank. The percentile ranks range from 1 to 99. If for example, the student's percentile rank on a given test is the 99th percentile, 99 percent of the students at that age or grade level nationally scored below that student. If the student's percentile rank or score is the 50th percentile, 50 percent of the students at that age or grade level scored below that student. If the student's percentile rank is 2nd, only two percent of the students at that age or grade level nationally scored below that student. Scores below the 25th percentile are considered below average; scores slightly below the 50th percentile and slightly above the 50th percentile are considered average; scores above the 75th percentile are above average.

Another way in which scores are compared to the national norm group is through the use of stanines. The word "stanine" means standard nine. It is a way of comparing the performance of the student to the national norms, where stanines 1, 2, and 3 are below average, stanines 4, 5, and 6 are average; and stanines 7, 8, and 9 are above average.

Intelligence test scores are compared to the norm group. The range for comparison is from 55 to 145 and above. Below average scores range from 55 to 85, average is from 86 to 114, above average is from 115 to 129, superior is from 130 to 145, and genius is 146 and above. Qualitative terms are often used in place of or in addition to quantitative terms when presenting or discussing the results of an intelligence test. An important consideration is that most psychologists and psychometrists believe that intelligence is not static.

Grade equivalent scores have been used in discussing norm-referenced tests in the past and are still used in some cases today. However, they are discouraged by many groups which are knowledgeable about testing. In standardized group testing, students are generally given a test booklet at their grade level. With a test booklet at his/her grade level, a student can only do well or poorly at that grade level. However, when grade equivalent scores are used for comparing and reporting student scores, below average, average, and above average are represented by grade levels. As an example, if a fifth-grade student was evaluated on a test designated for a fifth-grade student, he/she might receive a grade equivalent of second-grade if his/her performance was very poor. If he/she did very well on such a test, he/she might receive a grade equivalent score of eighth grade.

However, in the first case, it would not mean that the fifth-grade student had a second-grade reading level, nor would it mean that the student who received a grade equivalent of eighth grade was on the eighth-grade reading level. Rather, it would mean that the fifth-grade student who received a second-grade level score read very poorly for a fifth-grade student reading material designated for the fifth grade. As in the case of the student who received an eighth-grade rating while reading the material designed for fifth grade, his/her rating would mean that he/she read the selection very well. Using the ratings of below average, average, and above average, in the case of the fifth-grade material, it could be said that a standing of first grade, second grade, or third grade would be below average, a standing of fourth grade, fifth grade, and sixth grade would be average, a standing of seven, eight, and nine would be above average. Only if the students were tested on multilevel materials, representing second through eighth grades, could the second-grade level equivalent or the eighth-grade level equivalent be valid grade standings.

In the case of the criterion-referenced test, the goal is to determine if a particular student or group of students have mastered the subject or content-area material at a predetermined level. The predetermined level for passing may be at the 80 percent level, or it may be at the level where the student is required to get three out of four items about a certain concept correct. Some educators find the criterion-referenced test to provide a better assessment of student performance than the norm-referenced test. However, neither the results of the criterion-referenced test nor the norm-referenced test are perfect. The academic value of achievement tests must be examined in light of a number of considerations that revolve around the imperfection of all tests.

All tests have errors in them. These errors may be caused by the phrasing of a sentence in a test in a way different from the way it was taught. Such an error could happen when a test designer uses an unfamiliar synonym in a question that would otherwise be familiar to the student. An error can be as simple as a student guessing at an answer and getting it right or a student blackening the wrong space on the answer sheet. An extremely important consideration in this matter is that no test is perfect based upon the fact that no test has perfect reliability. This concept is called the standard error of measurement. In a more technical book on testing there would be a formula for computing this concept. It is enough here to remember that there is no perfect test. There are also limitations to any test or assessment. For example, the test or test items may not represent the content that has been taught and learned in a classroom. This would mean that the teacher who made the test or those who select the test for students are penalizing the test-takers. Another very important consideration is that any achievement test—formal or informal—just examines a sample of academic behavior.

COMPLEMENTARY THEMES

In light of many of the topics that have been presented in this chapter, most of our current practices represent a kaleidoscope—changing phases or events—of assessment in our schools. However, not all of the changes encompass the knowledge that there are limitations in all testing, that the standard error of measurement is a crucial consideration in all test results, and that an achievement test is just a sample of academic behavior. Many samples are needed to have a valid assessment of a student. The complementary nature of many of the items and assessments discussed or implied here should be considered by educators. Some examples of the complementary items are:

- Informal tests complement formal tests. Informal tests which are designed by the teacher often are more valid for the student than formal tests because informal tests usually evaluate what has been taught. Informal test usually are compared with a preset standard—a criterion. For instance, if a student achieves 90–100%, he/she might earn an A; those with 80–89% earn a B, those with 70–79% earn a C, those who earn 60–69% earn a D, those with 59% or less earn an F. On the other hand, formal tests allow the teacher to compare the performance of his/her class with other students nationally. (In many cases formal tests norms allow the teacher to make local comparisons.)
- Some of the features of the objective tests have been incorporated into the subjective tests. As an example, many subjective tests or essays now include rubrics, checklists, analytic scoring, and holistic scoring.
- Qualitative measures are complemented by quantitative measures and vice versa. Many qualitative assessments have added quantitative features to make the evaluation more objective. Many quantitative measures have added qualitative features for clarity, such as the terms "poor" or "excellent" after a score.
- Criterion-referenced tests and norm-referenced tests are often used to complete the academic picture of a student. The results of criterion-referenced tests show whether or not the students have mastered the subject or content area at the predetermined level, and the results of the norm-referenced tests show how the performance of the students compares with other students at that age or grade level nationally.
- Authentic assessments complement traditional assessments. Traditional assessments measure knowledge and comprehension usually on a paper-pencil type test or through teachers' oral questions. Authentic assessments represent "real world" evaluations such as journals, portfolios, science logs, books, inventions, and other creative projects. This type of assessment shows the application of knowledge, extension of knowledge, or even creative use of knowledge. In addition, in authentic assessment, the student examines the parts—analysis—and the pulling together of parts or information for the examination of the whole—synthesis.

The testing pendulum is swinging. There is the use of a potpourri of assessments to complete the assessment profile of a student. There is also a trend to clarify features of one type of assessment with features of another. Using some of the features of the objective test to clarify subjective essay writing not only makes such writing easier to score but makes grading more understandable to the student and makes the essay test grading more reliable. Using a rubric or analytic scoring, two evaluators or teachers should arrive at the same or very similar scores for an essay. Even though many parents and new educators often do not know the measurement and measurement terminology for talking about the fallibility of tests, they should understand that no test is perfect.

Many of the current classroom practices incorporate ongoing assessment in an effort to have many samples of all students' work. These assessments are on a continuum from the very informal such as classroom observations of students to formal assessments.

Most educators know that results from many different types of tests hold the key to unlock changes in learning and teaching. They realize that any tests just assesses a sample of behavior and that learning is not static.

While many educators are adhering to best practices and the knowledge that tests can be fallible; a number of pervasive current practices ignore the positions of many prestigious, well-respected education organizations and have turned a deaf ear to much of the assessment research. What is worse, many educators and legislators are using a single test to make major decisions. They have forgotten America's history of abuse and misuse of the formal objective tests. These concerns will be revisited in Chapters five, six, and seven.

REFERENCES

Alvermann, D. E. and Phelps, S. (1994). *Content Reading and Literacy*. Boston: Allyn and Bacon.

Anderson, W. (1990). *Read With Me: The Power of Reading—and How It Transforms Our Lives*. Boston: Houghton Mifflin Company.

Anastasi, A. (1976). *Psychological Testing*. New York: Macmillan.

Darling-Hammond, L.; Ancess, J.; Falk, B. (1995). *Authentic Assessment in Action*. New York: Teachers College Press.

Kozol, J. (1986). *Illiterate America*. Garden City, NY: Anchor Press/Doubleday.

Manzo, A. V. and Manzo, U. C. (1990). *Content Area Reading: A Heuristic Approach*. Columbus, OH: Merrill.

Popham, W. J. (1993). *Educational Evaluation*. Boston: Allyn and Bacon.

Roe, B.; Stoodt, B.; Burns, P. C. (1991). *The Content Areas, Secondary School Reading Instruction*. Boston: Houghton Mifflin.

Rothman, R. (1995). *Measuring Up: Standards, Assessment, and School Reform*. San Francisco: Jossey-Bass.

Rubin, D. (1991). "What a Teacher Should Know About Tests, Measurement, and Evaluation," in *Diagnosis and Correction in Reading Instruction*. Boston: Allyn and Bacon.

Schlechty, P. C. (1990). *Schools for the Twenty-first Century: Leadership Imperatives for Educational Reform.* San Francisco: Jossey-Bass.

Smith, C. B. (ed.) (1990). *Alternative Assessment of Performance in the Language Arts: Proceedings.* Bloomington, Indiana: ERIC Clearinghouse in Reading and Communication Skills and Phi Delta Kappa (Copublished).

Wiggins, G. P. (1999). *Assessing Student Performance. Exploring the Purpose and Limits of Testing.* San Francisco: Jossey-Bass.

CHAPTER FIVE

Viewing Achievement Tests Through the Eyes of Professional Organizations and Other Stakeholders

Student evaluation is basic to student growth. It demands careful, thoughtful attention. Yet what typically passes for student evaluation, what fills the public discourse, is an overarching model of assessment, built around a host of standardized tests, that doesn't provide teachers with much information of consequence.

VITO PERRONE

As the assessment pendulum swings, many educational organizations have examined themselves. Much of the examination comes from their concerns with the types of assessments, the designs, the usefulness of the results, changes in intervention based on the results, and other critical issues. Because of these concerns, many of these organizations have written new standards and position statements as they relate to assessments. As an example, the National Assessment of Educational Progress (NAEP) has decided to examine its past practices in an effort to " . . . provide more useful information about student achievement and the nation's educational systems to the community of educators, policy makers, and the public. . . ." These views were discussed in Pellegrino and other editors' (1999) edition of the book *Grading the Nation's Report Card: Evaluating NAEP and Transforming the Assessment of Educational Progress.* The book was a collaboration among the editors and the Committee of the Evaluation of National and State Assessment of Educational

Progress, Board of Testing and Assessment, Commission on Behavioral and Social Sciences and Education, and National Research Council.

The National Assessment of Educational Progress has been evaluating the performance of America's students for nearly 30 years. However, recently the organization felt the need to evaluate itself so that it can improve upon its efforts. Many other educational organizations have felt the need to restructure their work or to develop and present the group's position on some current assessment practices. Since assessment is an integral part of learning and the practice of education, both the examination of common learning theories and best teaching/learning practices seem to be a logical preface to the concerns. Key learning theories and best practices influence teaching and decision making. In this chapter, a number of standards and position statements of leading education organizations will be examined. Many of the positions of these leading education organizations critique assessment in general but especially the pervasive proficiency test. Also, where possible, the positions of parents— key stakeholders in education—will be presented.

There seems to be a consensus among professionals from different education organizations about the best assessments and assessment practices. These positions represent different subjects or content areas. An examination of the concerns of different content area organizations provides educators with a vantage point from which to work for needed changes in an effort to improve the teaching and learning experiences of America's children. Such examination will, thereby, provide ideas not only for improving assessment but for the learning and teaching experiences, approaches, and methods.

Talks and critiques of assessment are very commonplace in today's communities. This widespread topic of discussion has flourished because assessment among America's schools is the subject of newspaper and magazine articles. It is the topic of a widely published report card of each school as well as each school district's assessment progress. It is part of television news. It is part of parent-teacher meetings. It is part of church meetings. The topic seems to be an appropriate one for any time and any place. The results of many of the assessments are at the same time a source of fear and a source of pride. Such assessments are also a source of reward and punishment. The widespread publicity, the fear and pride, and the reward and punishment in relation to assessment are pervasive today because almost every state is adding another layer of formal achievement testing to its annual assessments in the name of the state proficiency tests. Most states say that the assessment is for student intervention and teacher accountability. However, a number of educators and parents question both. Needless to say, the new layer of testing is controversial.

Many of the current positions of leading national, education organizations

grow out of the knowledge that there are educational practices that foster learning and tests that complement learning and achievement. Usually the educational practices that foster learning and best test practices have come from
researchers and learning theorists. Researchers and learning theorists, past
and contemporary, have often advocated similar educational practices. Some
of these learning theories are:

- Active, participatory, integrated, student-centered learning is more effective than
  passive, teacher-centered learning.
- Early and ongoing substantive, clarifying, individualized intervention should be
  part of every school's program.
- Collaborative and cooperative learning are needed since they provide opportunities to share and weigh ideas of others and represent approaches used in the "real"
  world.
- Reading, writing, discussing, and higher-order thinking should be stressed in all
  content areas.
- Prior knowledge should be tapped or developed for each learning activity.
  Independent learning is a desired outcome in each content area.
- The process model of learning is student-centered and lets students focus on the
  "how" of problem solving while letting them understand that in many cases
  there are multiple plausible answers.
- Interest, motivation, attitudes, and multiple intelligences are important consid-
  erations in all learning experiences.
- Culture is reflected in most learning; multicultural education should be part of the
  teaching and learning experiences in every classroom.
- Learning is strategic.
- The teacher should be a coach or a facilitator rather than a dispenser of knowledge. The teacher's modeling of strategies such as directed-reading-thinking
  activities, read alouds, and think alouds facilitate student learning.
- Multiple tools should be used to integrate and to expand student learning. They
  should include such things as textbooks, newspapers, supplementary materials,
  trade books, out-of-grade books such as picture books. Computers should be used
  at all levels and in all content areas.
- *Assessment should be ongoing and include many samples of student behavior,
  acquired by formal and informal assessments, formative and summative assessments, projects, experiments, and creative work.*

The above learning theories, which reflect some of the ideas of America's leading learning theorists such as Ralph Tyler, who lived for almost a century from
1902 to 1994, and John Dewey, who lived almost a century from 1859 to
1952. They and others have provided the base for today's best practices for
teaching and learning and testing. The best practices flow from well-researched
theories. When applied in a judicious way and tailored by the teacher to the
individual classroom needs, these theories help prepare students for the twenty-
first century. Many of the best practices are just germinating. Some are complete. All will undergo revisions. All show the visions and insights of the

theorists. The aforementioned learning theories have become the framework for many current best practices. A few of the practices which are based on leading learning theories are:

- Learning is an active process. For this reason, students should be involved in planning and evaluating learning experiences where possible. There should be many application-type and hands-on activities. The goal is to help students learn to learn.
- Learning is goal oriented. The teacher along with the students should set and clarify the purpose. The purpose should be reviewed and reinforced in an ongoing way (formatively) as well as at the end of the learning activity or semester (summatively).
- Learning is meaningful. Prior knowledge should be developed, and predictions should be made before a learning experience or activity is begun. Questions and exploration for multiple meanings should be encouraged during the experience or activity. A few such activities would include having the students anticipate what will happen in a activity or reading selection. A second one is having the students think of what they know about a topic before beginning, having them state what they want to know or learn about the topic, and finally having them evaluate what they have learned from a topic. This is a strategy called K-W-L. In this strategy, students ask: **What do I *know*? What do I *want* to know? What did I *learn*?** In addition to developing prior knowledge and setting a purpose, it provides the students with a review of the topic or reading.
- Learning is strategic. Such strategies as helping the students understand and use a textbook effectively can be accomplished by utilizing an informal textbook inventory. This strategy helps to familiarize students with the features of books both fiction (narrative) and nonfiction (expository). This inventory, which is described in Chapter four, also helps students understand and use the organizational patterns of textbooks and learn how to extract information from charts, graphs, art work, and other items. Using the inventory students learn to evaluate books as well as learn new strategies for each content area.
- Learning activities should be developmentally appropriate and have **continuity**—providing opportunities for repeating the activities or experiences and continuing opportunities for practice. The learning activities should also have **sequence**—moving from the simpler to the more complex. Finally**, integration**—giving unity and wholeness to experiences and activities so that students can see how learning within a content is connected as well as being connected to learning outside the content—is crucial.
- The teacher should ensure that the learning is *interesting* to the students. Student interest can be whetted by: relating the learning to enjoyable student experiences such as a popular student magazine, encouraging lively student discussion of a learning experience or activity, using teacher-developed games, asking the students to collaborate with their teacher or with their peers in making an appropriate content game. Whetting their interest is very important with contemporary students.
- Diversity in culture and language should be expected and capitalized on in the changing school. Multiculturalism should be represented in the adopted texts, other materials, and activities. The goal is that students be bicultural and bilingual and that activities foster respect between the students and teacher and among peers.

- Student involvement should be encouraged through reading, writing, discussion, thinking critically, and learning independently. This should be beyond required assignments and should occur across the curriculum.
- Student collaboration should be built into activities by having group brainstorming, peer editing of writing activities, peer critiques of projects, conflict resolution strategies for discussions where there are differences of opinions. Student-teacher conferences should also be part of this collaboration. Interdisciplinary terms and concepts should be compared and contrasted across the curriculum.
- The teacher should serve as a coach or facilitator. This will allow for a great deal of interaction to take place so that students experience a collaborative, cooperative classroom. Such classrooms may be top down where the teacher is the leader, some may be bottom up where the students are the leaders, but most often they should be interactive where the teacher and students collaborate.
- The teacher needs to construct the learning experiences and activities so that a great many of them involve modeling or observation-type learning. This could be done through teacher or student demonstration of a learning activity such as how geometric dimensions and scales are used to construct a model of a house or room. There should be learning experiences and activities that involve discovery learning or heuristics. This could be done by having the student invent something or create a song, a poem, a story, a collage, a drawing. There should be times when receptive learning occurs by having either the teacher or the student be the provider of information. Multiple intelligences should be tapped as well as different learning styles and multi-method approaches. Such approaches capitalize on the uniqueness of each student.
- The teacher should know the students and capitalize on the strengths, motivations, and interests of the students. It is important to find, create, or discover what is relevant and liked by them. The teacher should also know what is irrelevant or disliked by students so that these things can be avoided if possible or in some way ameliorated if they are a necessary evil.
- The teacher should provide scaffolding for learning experiences or activities which are new or very difficult. Scaffolding provides students or learners with a great deal of academic support initially but less and less support as students begin to gain independence. The support could be in the form of a read-aloud, a think-aloud, a demonstration on how to begin a project, or any other enriching activity.
- The teacher should encourage independence through self-assessment. Such assessment is nurtured by directing each student to think about his/her own thinking. The thinking about one's own thinking or metacognition is the first and probably the most powerful form of assessment. Student-developed and teacher-developed checklists or open-ended or rhetorical questions should be posed to a student designer, relating to his/her work, project, invention, or creation. These practices foster critical thinking and independence.
- The teacher should encourage students to do real adult projects by collaborating on teacher-student research. This can be done by submitting papers and books for publication, by inventing new items, or by making innovative changes on existing or extant items.
- The teacher should provide experiences so that students understand how tests or assessments—teacher-made (informal), standardized (formal), and authentic—are developed. The purpose and interpretation of tests should be shared. The fact that there are no perfect tests should be part of the students' "test know-how." They

should also be taught effective test-taking strategies, which are reinforced on a regular basis. Further, they should also be encouraged to use self-evaluation or metacognitive skills on a regular basis to help them develop a critical view of their own work.

The above considerations for the classroom incorporate assessment to some degree, whether using very, very informal assessment such as observation, doing ongoing evaluation when solving a problem or creating a project, or taking a formal test such as the Iowa Test of Basic Skills or the Scholastic Aptitude Test. Also, self-assessment or metacognition should be included in each activity.

Similarly, best practices unfold from many of the current learning theories. The power of ongoing assessment—self-assessment (metacognition), informal, authentic, and formal—is supported by best practices. When used in a balanced, coordinated way the above forms of assessment support each other. Recently, however, formal testing has been front and center in the minds of students, parents, teachers, and the community. The best known and most-discussed of the current tests is the formal state proficiency test. As will be shown later in this chapter and in Chapter seven, the pervasive high-stakes state-proficiency test is neither aligned with best practices of key education organizations or with fairness in testing.

Research and best practices lead to enriched classroom learning environments, where assessment is a tool of learning that comes in multiple forms. These multiple forms of assessment can further academic growth and achievement. In the modern nurturing learning environment, the teacher is seen as a coach or facilitator, not the dispenser of knowledge as once was the view. The students are active and strategic. They are independent thinkers who can learn from text as well as multiple other sources including the Internet. They can learn from near and far peers or even by distance learning. They learn that there are multiple ways of learning that should include observation and discovery learning. They are collaborators. They are assessors. They learn that assessment must start with self assessment, be ongoing, and include multiple types of assessments. Students learn that neither learning nor assessment is perfect. While one student may best learn by one method, approach or strategy; others may learn by different methods, approaches, strategies, and assessments.

Many professional education organizations have looked at assessment as an important part of learning. Like the National Assessment of Educational Progress, they see formal assessment as a vital part but not the whole of the learning process. In addition, some organizations such as the International Reading Association (IRA) think that the formal, informal, and authentic assessments all complement each other—they stress the use of multiple indices. As early as 1979, the International Reading Association (IRA) adopted the following position. In presenting the position statement or statements and standards of major education organizations in this chapter, quotations rather than summaries are used so that the reader is looking at primary statements. They are reprinted here with the permission of the author and publisher.

No single measure or method of assessment of minimum competencies should ever be the sole criterion for graduation or promotion of a student. Multiple indices assessed through a variety of means, including teacher observation, student work samples, past academic performance, and student self-reports should be employed to assess competence.

Furthermore, every effort should be made through every possible means to remediate weaknesses diagnosed through tests. Retention in grade or non-promotion of a student should be considered only when all other available methods have failed.

For these reasons, the Board of Directors of the International Reading Association is firmly opposed to the efforts of any school, state, provincial or national agency which attempts to determine a student's graduation or promotion on the basis of any single assessment (The Reading Teacher, 1979).

Concerned about the information that traditional assessments were not providing, the International Reading Association and the National Council of Teachers of English published a document which outlined the *Standards for Assessment of Reading and Writing* in 1994:.

Standard 1: The interests of the students are paramount in assessment.
Standard 2: The primary purpose of assessment is to improve teaching and learning.
Standard 3: Assessment must reflect and allow the critical inquiry into curriculum and instruction.
Standard 4: Assessment must recognize and reflect the intellectually and socially complex nature of reading and writing and the important roles of school, home, and society in literacy development.
Standard 5: Assessment must be fair and equitable.
Standard 6: The consequences of an assessment procedure are the first and most important consideration in establishing the validity of the assessment.
Standard 7: The teacher is the most important agent of assessment.
Standard 8: The assessment process should involve multiple perspectives and sources of data.
Standard 9: Assessment must be based in the school community.
Standard 10: All members of the educational community—students, parents, teachers, administrators, policy makers, and the public—must have a voice in the development, interpretation, and reporting of assessment.
Standard 11: Parents must be involved as active, essential participants in the assessment process.

National Council of Teachers and the International Reading Association Task Force on Assessment (1994) *Standards for Assessment of Reading and Writing,* pp. 13–37. Reprinted with permission.

In the December 2003/January 2004, issue of *Reading Today*, the International Reading Association responded to the recent flat scores of students taking the National Assessment of Educational Progress test by saying " . . . All too often politicians want to test rather than invest; testing for every level of government, while yielding almost no data that helps (sic) instruction."

According to the standards of the International Reading Association and the Council of Teachers of English, many designers of state proficiency tests and a number of other formal tests do not consider that (1) the interests of the students are a crucial consideration in this assessment, (2) their assessment seems to drive the curriculum rather than leading to improved teaching and learning—especially critical inquiry, (3) validity and the validation process should be priorities in the test development stages of the assessment, (4) the assessment needs to be based on the school community, (5) the teacher should be used as an agent of the assessment, and (6) all the stakeholders should be included in all decision-making processes about this assessment.

In the area of science the National Science Foundation (NSF) has stated that science is active and requires active assessment. Aligned with this organization, George Hein (1991) stated in *Expanding Student Assessment* that "Science is an active process that involves using physical skills, imagination, and creativity to tackle the usually ill-defined problems and events of the real world." Hein felt that having the students find the correct answer from questions on a multiple-choice test is rather ridiculous. In 1987, a group of supportive curriculum developers of the National Science Foundation made the following statement in regard to assessment in the area of science:

> Research shows that extant achievement tests do not measure the broad range of scientific processes or higher order thinking skills, nor do they give insight into naive versus "scientific" interpretation of phenomena. All these domains are integral to current approaches to teaching and learning science. . . . On the contrary, because the emphasis of these norm-referenced tests is on types of questions that can be answered by simple recall of facts, and/or recognition of textbook experiments, they mitigate against the less predictable hands-on approach. . . . . The existing norm-referenced tests not only fail to support or encourage the implementations of new developments in science curriculum and pedagogy, but their continued, near-universal use may dampen or totally inhibit implementation of such approaches. Thus, there is a need for alternatives to existing national, norm-referenced tests. The alternatives must be of high quality and must meet the public's needs for accountability and comparability across programs and districts. Additionally, they must be congruent with the philosophy of science teaching and learning the National Science Foundation promotes. (Harmon 1988)

Similarly, S. Raizen and others, (1989), as a policy group of the National Center for Improving Science Education, presented a number of goals, including the following one for improving the assessment of science:

> Improvement Goal 2. Development of externally mandated assessments as well as class-
> room tests that conform closely to the characteristics of good science curricula and
> instruction. . . . Assessments should provide greater opportunities for children to
> interact with stimulus materials, (2) attend to understandings of constructs and prin-
> ciples as well as factual knowledge, (3) probe approaches to problem solving as well as
> outcomes, (4) be explicitly integrated with the curriculum and with instruction, (5)
> incorporate hands-on activities whenever feasible, and (6) be structured around group
> as well as individual activities. (Sena A. Raizen, author, and member of the National
> Center for Improving Science Education, J. B. Baron, A. B. Champagne, E. Haertel,
> I. N. V. Mullis, and J. Oakes. *Assessment in Elementary School Science Education,*
> Washington, DC. Reprinted with the permission of the lead author.)

The positions of the National Science Foundation and the National Center for Improving Science Education stress that the widely used, fact-oriented, multiple choice assessment does not conform to the hands-on experiences, problem solving, and critical thinking involved in science teaching, learning, and curricular design. Based on the science policies, goals, and statements, it would seem that the fact-oriented, multiple choice, science items on many of the state proficiency tests may be inadequate assessments for science.

As have many other education organizations and commissions, the National Commission on Testing and Public Policy (NCTPP) (1990) has examined educational assessment and stated:

> Testing programs should be redirected from over-reliance on multiple-choice tests
> toward alternative forms of assessment. . . .

> A major cause for the distortion of test results and the ill effects of testing over the last
> several decades has been that the same test, or kind of test, has been asked to serve many
> important but different functions. Therefore, we recommend that testing for different
> purposes be differentiated and disentangled. Specially, we urge the assessment of the
> effectiveness of social institutions. (National Commission of Testing and Public Policy.
> (1990), *From Gatekeeper to Gateway: Transforming Testing in America,* Chestnutt
> Hill, Massachusetts: National Board on Educational Testing and Public Policy, pp.
> 26–30. Reprinted with permission.)

Using the position statement of International Reading Association as a barometer, the National Commission on Testing and Public Policy's position is to avoid the use of a single assessment for major decision making by using multiple-types of assessments. The other national education organization groups seem to hold the same position.

A number of educators and researchers have critiqued the current use of the multiple-choice format of widely used assessments just as many of the science educators and researchers have. As an example, Sheila Valencia and P. David Pearson (April 1987) in an article in *The Reading Teacher* entitled "Reading Assessment: Time for a Change" have critiqued the current use of assessments. They acknowledged that comprehension is key in reading, whether it be in comprehension of vocabulary or the comprehension of text. They compared what we know about the reading process and how this new knowledge about comprehension is not reflected in what is measured and the way it is measured on standardized tests.

In Phillip Schlechty's (1990) book *Schools for the Twenty-first Century,* he voices his thoughts on tests and testing which seems to be in "sync" with the National Council of Teachers of English and the International Reading Associations' Standard 7. "The teacher is the most important agent of assessment."

> In my view, reading assessments—and most other assessments as well—should only be conducted when a teacher, or group of teachers, indicates a child is capable of doing well on the assessment. The purpose of the assessment should be to validate the teacher's judgment rather than to test the child's ability to read. From time to time diagnostic tests may be appropriate, but even these should be used sparingly and only when teachers believe the test will give them valuable information they do not have and cannot get in any other way. (p. 118)

Judah Schwartz (1991) has written a chapter entitled "The Intellectual Costs of Secrecy in Mathematics Assessment" in Perrone's *Expanding Student Assessment.* He states that neither the media, general public, nor the students who are tested on the currently used, standardized, norm-referenced tests receive reports on the performance on specific questions. Additionally, none of the above-mentioned stakeholders has received the questions nor do the media publish the questions upon which the performance is based; they merely see or hear about the end product. Schwartz feels that the stakeholders should have access to sample questions. Further, he stresses that test designers should have rich indexed data bases of problems and projects which also should be available to the public. He critiques the secrecy of mathematics assessment. Some paraphrases of Schwartz's thoughts are:

- Mathematics questions should allow for creativity and invention;
- Mathematic questions should not contrast explicitly with our (mathematics) pedagogic goals;
- Questions must not be wrong in areas of mathematics where we want students to be right;
- Questions must not be simplistic where we want students to discern and deal with complexity;
- Questions must be mathematically interesting.

The principles and standards of the National Association of Teachers of Mathematics seem to repeat the Schwartz's statements. The main assessment principle of this group is that "Assessment should support the learning of important mathematics and furnish useful information to both teachers and students." The following are some of this group's principles and standards:

> When assessment is an integral part of mathematics instruction, it contributes significantly to all students' mathematics learning. When assessment is discussed in connection with standards, the focus is sometimes on using tests to certify students' attainment, but there are other important purposes of assessment. Assessment should be more than merely a test at the end of instruction to see how students perform under specific conditions; rather, it should be an integral part of instruction that informs and guides teachers as they make instructional decisions. Assessment should not merely be done to students; rather, it should also be done for students, to guide and enhance their learning. (For all the mathematics standards: Reprinted with permission from *Principles and Standards for School Mathematics,* copyright 2000, by the National Council of teachers of Mathematics (NCTM). NCTM does not endorse the contents or validity of this book. All rights reserved. Standards are listed with the permission of the NCTM.)

Further, the National Council of Teachers of Mathematics in their 1995 book entitled *Assessment Standards for School Mathematics* presented the following six standards about exemplary mathematics assessment. These standards address how assessment should:

- reflect the mathematics that students should know and be able to do;
- enhance mathematics learning;
- promote equity;
- be an open process;
- promote valid inference;
- be a coherent process.

Other standards are presented, including the fact that assessment should enhance students' learning. Additionally, it is stated that:

> Research indicates that making assessment an integral part of classroom practice is associated with improved student learning.

> It is important that . . . teachers include attention to formative assessment in making judgments about teaching and learning.

> Good assessment can enhance students' learning in several ways. First, the tasks used in an assessment can convey a message to students about what kinds of mathematical knowledge and performance are valued. The message can in turn influence the decisions students make. . . .

> When teachers use assessment techniques such as observations, conversations and interviews with students, or interactive journals, students are likely to learn through the

process of articulating their ideas and answering the teacher's questions. Feedback from assessment tasks can also help students in setting goals, assuming responsibility for their own learning, and becoming more independent learners. . . . scoring guides, or rubrics, can help teachers analyze and describe students' responses to complex tasks and determine the students' levels of proficiency.

Assessment is a valuable tool for making instructional decisions. To ensure deep, high-quality learning for all students, assessment and instruction must be integrated so that assessment becomes a routine part of ongoing classroom activity rather than an interruption. In addition to formal assessments, . . . teachers should be continually gathering information about their students' progress through informal means, such as asking questions during the course of a lesson, conducting interviews with individual students, and giving writing prompts.

When teachers have useful information about what students are learning, they can support their students' progress toward significant mathematical goals. The instructional decisions made by teachers—such as how and when to review prerequisite material, how to revisit a difficult concept, or how to adapt tasks for students who are struggling or for those who need enrichment—are based on inferences about what students know and what they need to learn.

Assessment should reflect the mathematics that all students need to know and be able to do, and it should focus on students' understanding as well as their procedural skills.

To make effective decisions, teachers should look for convergence of evidence from different sources. Formal assessments provide only one viewpoint on what students can do in a very particular situation—often working individually on paper-and-pencil tasks, with limited time to complete the tasks. Over–reliance on such assessments may give an incomplete and perhaps distorted picture of students' performance.

Many assessment techniques can be used by mathematics teachers, including open-ended questions, constructed-response tasks, selected-response items, performance tasks, observations, conversations, journals, and portfolios.

When teachers are selecting assessment methods, the age, experience, and special needs of students should be considered.

When done well, assessment that helps teachers make decisions about the content or form (often called formative assessment) can also be used to judge students' attainment (summative assessment).

To maximize the instructional value of assessment, teachers need to move beyond a superficial "right or wrong" analysis of tasks to focus on how students are thinking about the tasks.

Whether the focus is on formative assessment aimed at guiding instruction or on summative assessment of students' progress, teachers' knowledge is paramount in collecting useful information and drawing valid inferences.

The principles, standards, and position statements of the National Council of Teachers of Mathematics seem to be congruent with those of other organizations of professional educators who have been presented in this chapter.

The position statements and standards of the National Council of Social Studies—their learning, teaching, and assessment standards—seem to be aligned with the other major professional education organizations. In addition to the alignment, the National Council of Social Studies has mentioned their adherence to the 1986 recommendations of the Carnegie Task Force on Teaching as a Profession for restructuring schools. This Council has stated that parallel to the restructuring of schools is the desire of transforming student assessment " . . . from an over-reliance on machine-scored standardized tests to approaches that balance such measures with alternatives such as performance assessments or authentic assessments. The design of such assessments reflects actual learning tasks such as speaking effectively or taking a reasoned stance on a controversial social issue. The focus is on the processes students use, not merely the answers they choose." Some of the other standards and position statements are found below:

> In this environment of shared instructional leadership and authentic assessment, the social studies teaching profession can enhance learning in history and social sciences and develop the skills necessary for participatory citizenship.
>
> A comprehensive evaluation plan for social studies includes appropriate use of both teacher-made achievement tests and standardized tests. The two types of tests serve complementary, sometimes overlapping purposes. Tests in social studies serve a number of purposes. Social studies teachers use tests:

- to determine the learning needs of students;
- to provide learners with information and assistance on their progress toward social studies objectives;
- to provide information for assigning grades and for making decisions about promoting students to the next grade level;
- to compare the social studies achievement of their students with those of a broad population of students.

As far as assessments, the National Council of Social Studies has stated that evaluation instruments should:

- focus on stated curriculum goals and objectives
- be used to improve curriculum and instruction
- measure both content and process
- be chosen for instructional, diagnostic, and prescriptive purposes
- reflect a high degree of fairness to all people and groups

Evaluations of student achievement should:

- be used solely to improve teaching and learning
- involve a variety of instruments and approaches to measure students' knowledge, skills, and attitudes
- be congruent with both the objectives and the classroom experiences of the students examined
- be sequential and cumulative

The overriding purpose of testing in social studies classrooms is to improve learning. To accomplish this goal, social studies teachers must be proficient in interpreting and reporting test results, including those from standardized tests. Standardized test data collected in social studies classrooms must be available to the teacher for study.

To gauge effectively the efforts of students and teachers in social studies programs, evaluators must augment traditional tests with performance evaluations, portfolios of student papers and projects, and essays focused on higher levels of thinking. The development of a comprehensive, systematic, and valid evaluation for a social studies program requires the creative cooperation of social studies professionals with educational measurement specialists. Ideally, evaluation design is integral to the curriculum development process and proceeds simultaneously with it. (The 1991 standards from National Council of Social Studies' "Testing and Evaluation of Social Studies Students." *Standards and National Council of Social Studies' Position Paper.* Washington, D.C.: National Council of Social Studies (NCSS) are reprinted with the permission of NCSS. NCSS does not endorse the contents or validity of this book.)

In examining the standards, principles, and position statements on assessment of the above professional organizations, there seems to be consensus among these organizations that represent varied subjects or content areas. Similarly, there are other stakeholders who have voiced concerns about the current use of the standardized tests—in many cases the culprit is the pervasive proficiency test. The proficiency tests are often called high-stakes tests because currently in many cases they are used singly to make major academic decisions such as retention of a student in a grade or denial of graduation for those students failing to pass the tests. (This is a practice that none of the leading professional education organizations supports.)

Other stakeholders who are in agreement with the professional education organizations are the parents. These parents, unfortunately, seldom have the benefit of a group or explicit knowledge of best educational practices. They do, however, have the implicit knowledge that helps them to view many of the current assessment or test practices as dangerous and damaging to students. On occasions, these stakeholders do join groups. This happened in the year 2000 when parents' opinions on a survey assessing standards and tests were reported as a group. The group administering the survey was the nonprofit nonpartisan organization Public Agenda. The survey was discussed in issue 30 of *Reading Today* (December 2000/January 2001) where the article stated that while parents were in favor of higher standards, they were opposed to having decisions made based on a single test. This is a rare example when parents' opinions were reported as a group. When parents join groups, what might have been a few, weak voices without the group grow to a crescendo which, in this case, loudly expressed their displeasure about the current practice of schools using a single test to make major decisions.

The concerns of these stakeholders are in their own way aligned with good practices and many of the principles, standards, and position statements of professional organizations. Many of the parents are joined by concerned citizens. In presenting a number of the concerns about assessment from these stakeholders, a disproportionate number of concerned people are from Ohio, my area of residence. The reason for this is that this very important group of stakeholders does not always have a forum. Sometimes—especially in periods of academic turmoil—they are heard as parts of television news or documentaries. Sometimes they are seen in the local newspapers. Many of the thoughts have found a voice in both local and national newspapers and magazines as well as local and national radio and/or television programs. Their thoughts seem to represent general concerns. A number of these concerns are presented below according to the category designated in the heading:

TEST APPROPRIATENESS

Under the newspaper headings "Ohio Proficiency Tests Need Revamping" (September 5, 2000) and "Tangled Test Results" (June 19, 2000) some of the following complaints and comments are made by parents and concerned citizens about the fourth-grade and sixth-grade proficiency tests:

- The fourth-grade proficiency test is a horrible example of a test.
- The reading level of the test is one which is higher than fourth grade.
- The math questions are too ambiguous.
- Teachers are often puzzled by what test items mean.
- The time limit of two and one-half hours for five days is more time than is required of many college students.
- According to the state plan at the fourth grade, the one test will determine whether a student fails. A parent compared this failure of students on one performance to a newspaper reporter being judged on just one column.
- Parents do not object to a test like the Stanford Achievement Test because it does not carry the baggage of the proficiency test.
- There is a question as to how the proficiency test could be the end-all-and-be-all of tests.

- One parent says, "If it (the state) mandates a statewide, one-size-fits-all test, the test must be fair and developmentally appropriate for fourth-graders."
- These tests produce "Tangled Test Results." In many communities only a little over half and sometimes fewer fourth-grade students pass the test. The percent of students who pass one of the subtests from year to year fluctuates and would suggest that comparable forms of the tests are not used.
- The question is asked "Can the state develop a valid, credible means of measurement?"

TEST EQUITY

In three other articles "Raising the Education Bar, Leaving the Barricades" (August 18, 1998) "Equal Testing in an Unequal World Ensures Failure" (January 13, 1999), and "Low-scoring Schools Passed over for Reading Funds" (Martin, January 15, 2000) some of the following issues are discussed:

- Many students have not had the essential educational experiences to achieve successfully in the schools.
- The inequitable use of testing will increase early dropouts and psychological injury to students who fail.
- The articles state that the use of uniformity and standards in testing do not consider that there are great variations or differences as far as textbooks, weekly quizzes and tests, educational tools such as technology, and motivated teachers from district to district.
- One concerned parent says, "When our state holds all students responsible in meeting educational proficiency standards, it in turn admits full responsibility in providing fair and equal representation and education for every student to do so—a responsibility both morally and legally that has yet to be met."
- Of the funds allotted to bolster reading scores in the state of Ohio, some went to the students who excelled, and some of the districts most in need of funds did not get the funds because of not applying or because of being slighted. Some who did not apply stated that they did not have the personnel to apply or they received the information too close to the deadline.

There also seem to be some indecision among those who manage the state-mandated test. On November 30, 2000, the Cleveland, Ohio, *Plain Dealer* headline read, "Tougher Student Testing Urged." (Ohlemacher, November, 30, 2000) On December 8, 2000, the *Plain Dealer* headline read, "Proficiency-test Panel Eases Up." (December 8, 2000)

HIGH-STAKES TESTS AND LEARNING

The author of the single article in this category on high-stakes testing and learn-

ing entitled "High-stakes Tests Stifle Learning" is both a parent and an educator. He outlines and critiques the current conditions in this area:

- Ohio is now moving from the high-stakes test designated as the ninth-grade test
  to an even more challenging new tenth-grade test—The Ohio Graduation Test.
- "The tests are tied to so-called standards that are nothing more than extensive lists
  of special pieces of information neatly packaged into separate subject domains."
- While educational funds are being cut and teachers are being laid off, the expen-
  diture of funds to create, distribute, score, and report the results of the high-stakes
  tests are increasing.
- Districts devote greater proportions of class time and outside-the-class time to
  preparing students by teaching to the test.
- The current approach is expedient and data-driven "standardized" learning.
- Young people must see education as more than a series of tests to be passed.
- Educators must see themselves as professionals rather than technicians.
- Parents and community members should seek reforms—especially on the politi-
  cally motivated No Child Left Behind Act.

(The above ideas were expressed by Robert Brownlee in his article "High-stakes Tests
Stifle Learning" appearing in the March 1, 2005, edition of the Cleveland Plain
Dealer.)

Parents and concerned citizens just like members of professional education
organizations are concerned about appropriateness, use, and equity in testing.
Many parents show that they are well aware that much required learning
occurs long before schooling begins. Testing must be based on teaching and
learning opportunities and experiences. The test items need to be clear—not
ambiguous—and grade-level appropriate. A one-size-fits-all test is not appropriate as a sole test. Knowing that any test is just a sample of behavior, many
parents stated that students' grades and teachers' evaluations should be part
of decisions about retention or denial of graduation. Further, they are aware
of the full responsibility of the state for fairness in funding and school
opportunities.

COLLECTIVE THOUGHTS AND IMPLICATIONS

In this chapter, the primary or position statements and standards of five major
content-area or subject-area organizations and other organizations have been
presented. These organizations are concerned with education, learning, teaching, and testing as they affect the opportunities for meaningful student learning. The following items are part of the themes that run through the principles,
standards, and position statements of these professional education
organizations:

- Assessment should be an integral part of teaching and learning;
- Assessment should be formal, informal, and authentic;
- Assessment should be ongoing—it should be both formative—during the time of study—and summative—at the end of study;
- Assessment should go beyond the traditional multiple-choice items and total reliance on paper-pencil tests;
- Assessment should reflect the best practices in each content area;
- There should be equity in testing;
- No single test should be used for major decision making; rather, multiple, different types of assessments should be used;
- There are limitations in all assessments.

Parents, as major stakeholders in the education of their children, seem to share the concerns of all of the above professional education organizations. All seem to say the same thing that the National Assessment of Educational Progress is both saying and practicing as outlined in *Grading the Nation's Report Card*. The National Assessment of Educational Progress is evaluating and transforming their assessment. It seems that this is what is needed in our current assessments, including proficiency testing. With this in mind, Chapter six discusses fairness in testing.

REFERENCES

Algeri, G. (January 13, 1997). "Equal Testing in an Unequal World Ensures Failure." Cleveland, OH: *Plain Dealer,* 10B.

Brownlee, R. (March 1, 2005). "High-stakes Tests Stifle Learning." Letter to the Editor, Cleveland, OH: Plain Dealer.

Harmon, M. J.; Mokros, J.; Dawson, G.; Hartwig, R.; Henderson, R.; Lowery, L.; Taylor, Z. (1988). "Comments on the Need for New Assessment Materials." Informal Document. Washington, DC: National Science Foundation.

Hein, G. (1991). "Active Assessment for Active Science." In Perrone, V. (ed.) *Expanding Student Assessment.* Alexandria, VA: Association for Supervision and Curriculum.

International Reading Association Task Force on Assessment. (1994). "Standards for Assessment of Reading and Writing." Newark, DE: National Council of Teachers of English and International Reading Association.

International Reading Association, *Reading Today.* (December 2003/January 2004). "Reading Scores Remain Flat," 21: 3, 5.

Lazear, D. (1999). *Multiple Intelligence Approaches: Solving the Assessment Conundrum.* Chapter 5: "New Standards: What Should We Be Looking For?" Tucson, AZ: Zephyr.

Martin, M. (January 15, 2000). "Low-Scoring Schools Passed over for Reading Funds." Cleveland, OH: Plain Dealer.

McCord, C .B. and Rahn. C. C. (September 5, 2000). "Ohio Proficiency Tests Need Revamping," Letter to the Editor, Cleveland, OH: Plain Dealer.

National Center for Improving Science Education. (1989). *Improvement Goals on State and Local Policies and Practices in the Science Curriculum, Science Teaching and Assessment.* Washington, DC: National Center for Improving Science Education.

National Commission on Testing and Public Policy. (1990). *From Gatekeeper to Gateway: Transforming Testing in America.* Chestnut Hill, MA: National Commission on Testing and Policy, 26–30.

National Council for Teachers of Mathematics. (1995). *Assessment Standards for School Mathematics:* Reston, VA: National Council for Teachers of Mathematics.

National Council of Teachers of Mathematics. (2000). *Principles and Standards for School Mathematics.* Reston, VA: National Council of Teachers of Mathematics.

National Council of Social Studies (1991). "Testing and Evaluation of Social Studies Students." *Standards and National Council of Social Studies' Position Paper.* Washington, D.C.: National Council of Social Studies.

Neill, D.; Median, J. (1989). "Standardized Tests: Harmful to Educational Health." *Phi Delta Kappan,* 70: 688–697.

Oehlbert, B. (August 18, 1998). "Raising the Education Bar, Leaving the Barricades." Letter to the Editor, Cleveland, OH: *Plain Dealer.*

Ohlemacher, S. (December 8, 2000). "Proficiency-Test Panel Eases Up." Cleveland, OH: *Plain Dealer,* 1A.

Ohlemacher, S. (November 30, 2000). "Tougher Student Testing Urged."Cleveland, OH: *Plain Dealer,* 1A.

Parents & Reading—Parents Speak Out on Standards. (December 2000/January 2001). *Reading Today,* 30.

Pellegrino, J. W.; Jones, L. R.; Mitchell, K. J. (eds.) (1999). *Grading the Nation's Report Card; Evaluating NAEP and Transforming the Assessment of Educational Progress.* Washington, DC: National Academy.

Perrone, V. (1991). "Moving Toward More Powerful Assessment." In Perrone, V. (ed.) *Expanding Student Assessment.* Alexandria, VA: Association for Supervision and Curriculum Development.

Popham, W. J. (1995). *Classroom Assessment: What Teachers Need to Know.* Boston: Allyn and Bacon.

Raizen, S.; Baron, J.; Champagne, A.; Haertel, E.; Mullis, I; Oaks, J. (1989). *Assessment in Elementary Science Education.* Washington, DC: National Center for Improving Science Education.

Rothman, R. (1995). *Measuring Up, Standards, and School Reform.* San Francisco: Jossey-Bass.

Schlechty, P. C. (1990). *Schools for the Twenty-first Century: Leadership Imperatives for Educational Reform.* San Francisco: Jossey-Bass.

Schwartz, J. (1991). "The Intellectual Costs of Secrecy in Mathematics Assessment."In Perrone,V. (ed.) *Expanding Student Assessment.* Alexandria, VA: Association for Supervision and Curriculum Development.

"Tangled Test Results." Editorial. (June 19, 2000). Cleveland, OH: *Plain Dealer,* 8B

Valencia, S. and Pearson, P. D. (April 1987). "Reading Assessment: Time for a Change." *The Reading Teacher.* 40: 726–732.

CHAPTER SIX

Analyzing the Qualities
of Fair Assessments

*" . . . We need to establish guidelines for the design of test to ensure
that the student's ability to justify or clarify a response is maximized."*
GRANT WIGGINS

The opening quotation is a good point upon which to begin this chapter—
"Analyzing the Qualities of Fair Assessments." The reason for this is because
it implies that there may be different viewpoints brought to a test item or items
by individual students. It also suggests that the teacher-learner relationship is
interactive. And that, a test or assessment is an integral part of learning.

Interaction in learning, inclusive of assessment, is very powerful. In the case
of informal tests, interaction between the student and teacher often takes place
during the review phase after the test has been taken by the student and
graded by the teacher. During this phase, a student or students may challenge
a teacher-expected answer and present strong support or rationale for their own
answer. This, in turn, may make the teacher weigh the student's answer and
revisit the initial expected response. At this point, the teacher may present a
very solid reason why the expected response is the accepted response. Or on
the other hand, the teacher may feel that the student has a valid point and agree
to accept the student's response as an acceptable answer. This is true interaction between the teacher and the student. In the case of formal assessment,
however, neither the teacher nor the student generally has an opportunity to

interact about the test since it is rare that the student gets to see the pool of test items again after the assessment has been administered and scored. In many school districts, the students' completed tests are returned to the publisher for scoring. After scoring, only the results, not the tests, are returned to the school district by the publisher. In the case of authentic assessments such as portfolios, journals, projects, and others, there may be interaction, between student and parent, the student and teacher, and the student and another student. Sometimes the interaction is to clarify or justify an answer.

Just as the student might find it vital to clarify an answer, clarity is the first of ten very important qualities of fair assessment. Other qualities which constitute fairness in assessment include (2) making sure that the test reflects new learning theories, research, and best test or assessment practices; (3) making sure that the assessment is objective; (4) assuring that formal tests are validated; (5) having the achievement test cover only items that the student has been taught and has had an adequate time to learn; (6) making sure the assessment is free of items that are biased against or biased for any student or groups of students; (7) making sure that reading or any other skill that is *not* intended to be tested in an item or subtest is kept to a minimum. (For example, a student's assessment in mathematics should not be overladen with the skill of reading. Adhering to this idea, a mathematics test should not include a test or subtest with all story problems. In such a case, the test may be measuring reading rather than mathematics.) The last three qualities are (8) assuring that an assessment program for any student contains multiple different types of assessments in order to get a holistic view of the student's achievement and to have comprehensive information for decision making; (9) evaluating the directions, items, and scoring to make sure that they are age and grade appropriate; and (10) viewing assessment through a lens that shows that there is an error in all measurement and that all assessment has limitations. Many of the above considerations are addressed in some way by the principles, standards, and position statements on assessment by the organizations that represent major content areas, which were presented in Chapter five. These ten qualities of fair assessment will be discussed in detail in the paragraphs below.

1. CLARITY

A crucial issue of any assessment is making sure that the test items, the directions, and the scoring are clear. This should mean that the directions and the items are written in plain, simple language and do not include ambiguous terms, challenging vocabulary, or technical terms that are not essential or central to the topic being tested. As an example, a simple sentence pattern where a single idea is developed should be used whenever possible in writing items and all directions since compound sentences where two main thoughts are joined together or other complex type sentences are more difficult to understand than simple sentences containing a single idea. Additionally, for each set of directions for each subtest, an example should be included to give students an opportunity to ask questions prior to beginning the subtest. Since items can be clear or unclear based on the viewpoint of the reader, it is wise to have a student or students from the grade level of the intended test to evaluate each test item as part of the validation process for a formal test or as a part of the initial preparation for informal and authentic assessments.

2. REFLECTION ON RESEARCH AND BEST PRACTICES

As mentioned throughout this book and re-emphasized in Chapter five, tests or assessments are integral parts of learning and should, therefore, be aligned with and complement research and best educational practices. This is the reason that tests are revised at regular intervals and that new editions are published. This is reflected in the National Assessment of Educational Progress's 1999 examination of its past practices with the desire to " . . . provide more useful information about student achievement. . . ." With this in mind, Sheila Valencia and P. David Pearson (1987) compared and contrasted what is known from research about the reading process with contemporary assessments. This, too, is among the critiques, principles, statements, and position statements of the leading national education organizations in America which were presented in Chapter five. These groups stress the fact that assessment must reflect the research and best practices in their particular content areas

3. OBJECTIVITY.

The name objective test represents a test or examination where there is one correct answer. This is why the test is called objective. Such tests are devoid of personal viewpoints. All test evaluators accept the same answer as the correct choice. This is a very important test quality when tests are designed for large segments of the population. The subjective element is eliminated.

As mentioned in Chapter one, in the past, essays and essay examinations were subjective. They are still widely used. Evaluation of the essay or essay test can be very subjective. What one evaluator thinks or thought was an outstanding or an A essay or essay test, another evaluator may think or may have thought was an average or C essay or essay test. However, the current use of rubrics and checklists that are shared in a pre-post fashion with both the teacher and student have made the essay or essay test almost objective. The rubric and checklist have taken much of the subjectivity out of the essay or essay test because the explicit standards for specified features are given along with the point value. Similarly, the checklist allows the student to revisit his/her essay or essay test to see that it includes the items on the checklist before he or she turns in the essay or essay test. The addition of the rubric and the checklist in a pre-post way have made the evaluation of essays a great deal fairer than it was in the past. The rubric and checklist add objectivity to the essay process. The quality of objectiveness is closely related to reliability and consistency.

4. VALIDATION

Objectivity, reliability, and consistency are part of the validation process. In Chapter two, the similarities and differences between the informal test and the formal test are discussed. In Chapter three, the validation process is outlined. The validation process of a test is one of checking or testing the test to determine whether a test measures what it says it does, i.e. is validity, and whether it measures the stated concept or concepts consistently, i.e. is reliability. Supporting the necessity of validation, George Hillocks, Jr. (2002) stated "The central problem in testing is knowing whether a test does what its proponents claim it does or not." This, of course, is part of validation. It is the validation process that separates the informal test from the formal test.

While there are numerous types of validity that a new test can be checked for, the most important one is content validity. Content validity can be checked by having experts in the content area of the test review and critique it. The experts' evaluations are compared and a percent of agreement is determined. Another way to determine content validity is to compare the contents of numerous textbooks in the subject area or content area and on the grade level of the test to determine the percent of agreement of the contents of textbooks with the contents of the test.

Another form of validity that may be checked is face validity—checking to see that the test looks like a test as far as format. References in the test items and the artwork should reflect contemporary culture so that they are both meaningful to the students. Concurrent validity is determined by comparing student test scores from the new test with an established validated test on the same content. When comparing the scores of students participating in the testing of the test—the validation—the scores of these students on the new test may be compared with scores on an existing established validated test. As an example, if the new test is an achievement test, the test designer might compare it with a test like the California Achievement Test or the Iowa Test of Basic Skills. There are other forms of validity. Criterion-related validity is one such form. Criterion-related validity is determined by comparing a student's performance on a test with the actual skill or task. As an example, a reading test might be compared with the actual task or skill of reading. If a student is outstanding in all aspects of reading in classroom and home reading experiences, it is expected that he/she would perform at an outstanding level on a paper-pencil test as reflected by his/her high scores. Still another validity is construct validity. Construct validity is determined by comparing the performance of the same student in similar areas such as intelligence and aptitude. The final type of validity is predictive validity. In predictive validity, the performance on a new test is used as a prediction of the success of some future performance such as a student's learning to read or his/her future success in college.

Part of the validation of the test is checking the new test for reliability. The three types of reliability are usually test-retest reliability, alternate-form reliability, and split-half reliability. As the name implies, in test-retest reliability, the new test is taken twice by each student in the validation group. The test is taken and then after a predetermined interval, the test is taken again. In the case of the alternate-form reliability, two equivalent forms of the new test are taken by each student. These scores are then compared. In split-half reliability, the answers on the new test are essentially split or divided into two parts—even and odd test items. The scores from the two parts are compared for consistency.

Through the process of validation—testing of the test—the newly-developed test is usually improved/refined by having people in the field—professional educators such as college professors and teachers and university graduate students who may also be professional educators—and students evaluate the test. Student input is secured when small groups of students participate in pilot studies where they take and receive a score on the test and then discuss the new test with the test designer. (The score is for the purpose of evaluating or improving the test, not for giving the student credit or for placing the score on the student's school record.) Then the input of the participating educators and students from the pilot study is used for the purpose of improving and refining the test.

The validation process improves the test. If it is done well, it can produce an excellent evaluation tool. However, even with a very thorough validation study, a perfect test cannot be produced. Since there are no perfect tests, various types of assessments have to be used to get a nearly holistic picture of the student. The fact that many people were using imperfect tests, as if they were perfect, prompted Oscar Buros to develop a yearbook called the *Mental Measurement Yearbook*. In the yearbook new and revised tests were and still are evaluated, especially to examine and critique the validity and reliability results of new tests or new editions of an old or established test. Since Oscar Buros first printed the *Mental Measurement Yearbook* in 1938, others have developed additional volumes to evaluate tests. One new set of volumes is entitled *Test Critiques*. Both the *Mental Measurement Yearbook* and Keyser and Sweetland's (1984) *Test Critiques* are currently in use. Oscar Buros' reason for developing the yearbook was to help educators and others to select tests or assessments by the value of the test. Questions such as the following were undoubtedly asked: Is the test a good test of math or reading or any other subject? Are the results consistent? If it is a well-validated test, the possibility that the test can correctly evaluate students is greatly increased. Oscar Buros found that in 1938, educators and others often chose tests by the way the test looked. This is face validity. While face validity is important, it is only one reason among a great many extremely important reasons for choosing a test for a large group of students. Chapter seven will discuss this topic from another perspective.

5. CORRELATION WITH CURRICULUM

Having the achievement test cover only items that the student has been taught and has had an opportunity to learn are at the heart of fairness of a test. Achievement tests by their very name imply that a concept, subject, or skill that has been taught and learned is being assessed. Since teaching and learning are integral to testing, opportunities to learn must be part of the assessment equation. Learning is on a continuum where a concept, subject, or skill is introduced, is taught, has an incubation period, and is reinforced, and is evaluated often. For permanent learning the concept, subject, or skill should be reviewed and retaught often, should be reinforced, and where needed should be remediated. The goal of such teaching is that the student will master the concept, subject, or skill being taught and will gain independence in it. That is, he/she will be able to use the information on his/her own, without the aid of the teacher.

Along the way, there should be informal tests including teacher observation, authentic student assessments including projects, lab reports, portfolios, journals, and many other "real life" experiences. There should be a considerable amount of informal and authentic testing before a student is required to take a formal test. Of course, this fairness certainly means that students have books, materials, experiences, access to the Internet, and any other opportunities that would help them learn in a meaningful, permanent way. Roger Farr (1986) in *Reading: What Can Be Measured?* said the following about reading which probably applies to all testing, "The most obvious one (the indicator of appropriateness of a test to an educational program) is that the skills measured by the test be those which were taught in the reading program and that those factors deemed constituents of reading behavior by the reading program be so considered by the test in about the same proportion. . . . It is logical that the measurement of growth would be invalid if the testing instrument failed to measure what has been taught."

Similar to Roger Farr, Phillip Schlechty (1990) in *Schools for the Twenty-first Century* said, " In my view reading assessments—and most other assessments as well—should only be conducted when a teacher, or group of teachers, indicates a child is capable of doing well on the assessment. The purpose of the assessment should be to validate the teacher's judgment rather than to test the child's ability to read." One of the important qualities of fairness of an achievement test is that a student be given many opportunities to learn in many different ways what is to be tested. This is not to say that students should not be asked to make predictions or extend what has been taught. Certainly, students should have opportunities to make predictions, to extend knowledge, and even to create or invent new ways of thinking and/or new inventions or projects.

6. UNBIASEDNESS

Items that contain references that may be biased against some students or biased for other students should be omitted from tests. Test publishers try to eliminate bias. Teachers, too, should eliminate bias from informal tests. References in test items to experiences that may be in the repertoire of some students but not in the realm of experiences for others would be biased against those who do not have these experiences as part of their backgrounds and biased for those who do have the experiences. A good example of this would be the use of sports metaphors or analogies. Experiences that wealthy students are likely to have and poor students are unlikely to have often influence the answer that the student gives or chooses. Questions or items are unfair that refer to airplane trips, experiences at Disney World or Disney Land, extensive allusions to farming, or any other reference or metaphor that would have been experienced by some students but not others. To be fair test items should contain no reference that is biased against some and biased for others because of race, religion, gender, socioeconomic level or beyond the realm of experience of some students.

7. APPROPRIATENESS OF SKILLS AND VOCABULARY

Skills or special vocabulary or technical words that are not related to the item being tested should be avoided. If the test is on mathematics, the test designer should avoid excessive use of story problems. If most or all of the items are couched in story problems, the examiner or teacher may not be able to separate the effect of the reading on the mathematics. If there are some story problems which the student misses but equally difficult abstract problems involving only computation which the student gets right, the teacher might speculate that the student has some difficulty with reading. The teacher's speculation could then be checked. Similarly, if there is special or technical vocabulary that is not related to the item being tested, this too should be avoided. A student who knows the answer but may not know the technical words or special vocabulary might miss the item because he/she does not know the unrelated vocabulary. To be fair, it should be clear what is being tested.

8. MULTIPLE ASSESSMENTS

In order for assessment of a student to be fair, it should be based on multiple different types of assessments. The needed multiple assessments include informal, formal, and authentic assessments and would provide a holistic view of students' comprehensive performance for decision making. The use of multiple assessments is aligned with current learning theories which recognize the uniqueness of student learning as discussed in the accounts of the ways that students learn through different modes—receptive (being told); observation (watching); and/or discovery/heuristic (doing/exploring).

It is also aligned with the pervasive theory of multiple intelligences as discussed by Howard Gardner and others. The use of multiple assessments is also supported by all of the major American education organizations as discussed in Chapter five. These organizations include the International Reading Association, the National Council of Teachers of English, the National Commission on Testing and Public Policy, the National Center for Improving Science Education, the National Science Foundation, the National Association of Teachers of Mathematics, the National Council of Teachers of Social Studies, the Carnegie Task Force on Teaching as a Profession, and among the members are: theorists, researchers, and teacher-practitioners. The use of multiple assessments is a crucial part of fairness in testing. This approach to assessment provides different opinions as well as complementary ways of looking at the student's performance from a myriad of perspectives. It also capitalizes on the student's preferred learning style and taps into the interests of the student.

9. APPROPRIATE SKILLS AND LANGUAGE

Directions should be clear and easy to read. They should not just be clear according to adult standards and the rules of standard English but clear to the student population who will need to read and interpret them. Where possible an example should be given so that students not only have the verbal directions but a model to follow. If the directions are unclear, items that a student may know may be answered incorrectly, which would be a test error rather than a student error. In addition, if the items have different point values assigned to them, this should be explained in the general directions as well as in the specific directions for the items. The items themselves should be clear and straightforward and should not have what Grant Wiggins (1999) points out in *Assessing Student Performance* as a "got ya" or "psyched you" mentality.

As mentioned earlier, Roger Farr in *Reading: What Can Be Measured?* points out that items which are fair are based on what has been taught and tested in the same proportion as the material was stressed in the teaching. As example, an item that was never stressed in class or one which is of little importance to the learning of the subject probably is not a fair item to include in the test. So fairness would mean that items included in the pool of test items are important to the subject, have been taught, and have been stressed. As pointed out earlier in this chapter, the wording and examples should be age and grade appropriate. A student should not be penalized because he/she did not know an irrelevant technical or special word which causes him/her to miss an item that is clearly known.

10. TEST LIMITATIONS

It is very important to view any test as a sample of behavior and further to view the sample as one that is far from perfect. Every test designer, teacher, administrator, and student should be made aware that all measurement, assessment, and/or tests have errors in them. This includes formal tests where the test itself is tested before administering the test to groups of students for a grade or evaluation. Clinton Chase (1974) states in *Measurement for Educational Evaluation* that errors may be inadvertently built into the test by the test designer. Errors may add to or subtract from the student's score. They may include such things as the student guessing and getting the answer correct; this is an error because the test is designed to assess what has been learned, not what can be guessed. For a number of reasons, the student may know the answer but get it wrong. One reason that this may happen could be because during the test the student had a mental block about the information, or the student may have inadvertently marked the wrong space even though he/she knows the correct answer.

In addition, any test and particularly the achievement test as discussed in this book has limitations. Some of the limitations are presented below:

- The items in an achievement test represent just a sample of the items that were part of the instructional program.
- Students may know many skills and be able to apply and synthesize much of the information; however, much of what they know may not be included in the test.
- The preparation of students for testing may cause the teacher to exclude items that are of great interest to the students and that could encourage them to explore the subject independently, critically, and creatively.

Further, Clinton Chase says, "They (achievement tests) should be interpreted in the context of all other data. Too often, achievement-test results are interpreted as the major, if not the only, valid source of information about how our children are doing. Clearly, this is wrong. General-achievement tests are broad surveys of skills. They do not provide the diagnostic clues that well-written, teacher-made tests can reveal." Chase's views are well aligned with the statements of the major American education organizations, which also point out the limitations of such assessments. To be fair to students, single achievement tests must be considered as only a sample of behavior.

CONSIDERATIONS

Even though few tests allow students to justify or clarify their responses, according to Grant Wiggins' quotation that starts this chapter, such justification is imperative. However, a number of the types of assessments that should be part of a total assessment of a student's academic performance do allow the student to clarify and justify his/her answer. Projects and writing assignments seem to fall into this category. One test that generally does not allow the student to clarify or justify his/her answer is the formal achievement test. Other assessments such as the informal, teacher-made test and authentic achievement assessments such as portfolios do permit the student the opportunity to clarify and justify his/her answer. The opportunity for students to clarify or justify an answer makes the assessment a great deal fairer than those that do not permit this.

Other considerations when analyzing the qualities of a fair assessment or assessment programs include (1) clarity of the assessment, (2) test items and test design that represent new learning theories, research, and best test or assessment practices, (3) assessments that are objective, (4) formal tests that are thoroughly validated, (5) assurance that items represent material that has been covered in class and that the student has had an adequate time to learn, (6) items that neither show bias against or bias for any student, (7) avoidance of items that are overladen with skills not being tested by the item but which may influence the student's score, (8) multiple differentiated assessments that are to be used for decision making and to get a holistic view of the student's achievement, (9) assurance that directions, scoring, and items are age or grade appropriate for the students taking the test and, (10) the acknowledgment that there is an error in all measurement and that all assessment has limitations. The aforementioned qualities of assessment and any others that provide the teacher and student with information that shows an accurate, holistic view of the student's performance represent fairness in testing.

Unless the class teacher is aware of the qualities of a fair test and the proper use of tests, he/she may incorrectly evaluate the results. The following scenario of a college professor, that he shared with his class, supports this statement. At the beginning of the school year, the professor had received glowing notes about how well his second-grade son read. However, after the teacher had administered, scored, and analyzed the results of a formal standardized test, she sent notes home, stating that his son had a reading problem. At a scheduled teacher-parent conference, the professor asked the teacher if she trusted her own judgment. Her response was that she thought his second grader did read well until he did poorly on the standardized test. The professor asked the teacher to recall the events of the testing day. The teacher said that on the test day after reading the directions, she told the second graders that the students who finished the test first could go out to the playground. As it turned out, his son was more interested in playground activities than the test. There was nothing wrong with his reading. The teacher should have known the importance of following the standardized test directions exactly and of not adding her own motivator—playground activities. As important, the teacher should have known about criterion-related validity in which a test is compared with the person's performance on the actual skill or task. And, she should have known that a test should validate her class experiences and observations of the professor's son. Her initial assessment was more powerful than the single standardized test results! Understanding the concepts, development, use, qualities of fairness, and limitations of tests are crucial for teachers and all stakeholders.

REFERENCES

Buros, O. K. (1938–2003). *The Mental Measurement Yearbooks*. Highland Park, N.J.: Gryphon Press (1938–1978) and Lincoln, NE: University Nebraska Press (1985–2003).

Chase, C. I. (1974). *Measurement for Educational Evaluation*. Reading, MA: Addison-Wesley.

Farr, R. (1986). *Reading: What Can Be Measured?* Newark, DE.: International Reading Association.

Hillocks, G., Jr. (2002). *The Testing Trap*. New York: Teachers College Press.

Keyser, D. J. and Sweetland, R. (eds.) (1984–2003). *Test Critiques*. Kansas, MO: Test Corporation of America (1984–1988). Austin, TX: PRO-ED (1991–2003).

Schlechty, P .C. (1990). *Schools for the Twenty-first Century, Leadership Imperatives for Educational Reform*. San Francisco: Jossey-Bass.

Valencia, S. and Pearson, P. D. (April 1987). "Reading Assessment: Time for a Change." *The Reading Teacher*. 40:726–732.

Wiggins, G .P. (1999). *Assessing Student Performance, Exploring the Purpose and Limits of Testing*. San Francisco: Jossey-Bass.

CHAPTER SEVEN

Visiting Achievement Test Misuses and Abuses

The extent to which children (learners) can acquire a given skill depends on the complex of abilities and experiences they bring to the learning situation.

CLINTON J. CHASE

Both the quotations from Clinton Chase (1974) in Chapter six and the epigraph introducing this chapter are extremely important considerations in avoiding achievement test misuses and abuses. Chase's central concern as voiced at the top of this page is that often the importance of students possessing the "complex of abilities and experiences" as a basis for acquiring new learning is forgotten.

Chase echoes educators who are troubled by some of the current and past standardized-test practices. However, there are a number of other negative practices that have led to misuses and abuses of standardized achievement tests and their results. Some other serious concerns include: (1) failing to recognize the uniqueness of each student, (2) not weighing all the variables that affect student learning and test-taking situations, (3) not using past and present critical research results to support test uses and decision making, and (4) allowing lay persons outside the field of education to make decisions that are influenced by economics and politics rather than research findings, best teaching and learning practices, and the best interest of students. Often legislators' desire for accountability at the risk of violating research findings and best practices in learning, teaching, and testing has put undue pressure on teachers, parents, and students and too little emphasis on meaningful learning.

USE OF FORMAL ACHIEVEMENT TESTS AS THE ONLY SOURCE OF STUDENT INFORMATION

Clinton Chase's remarks cited in Chapter six echo the voices of all major American education organizations as stated very explicitly in their principles, position statements, and standards. These educators have clearly, loudly, and unanimously voiced the idea that it takes many different types of assessments to come up with a holistic view of a student's performance that can then be used for educational decision making. Further, the members of these major American education organizations and their leaders are well versed through their studies and experiences with various assessments and, therefore, are good spokespersons in this area. They are familiar with the concept that there is an error in all measurement—the standard error in measurement. What is more important, they know that some formal tests are fair, some are good, some are outstanding, but none is perfect. Additionally, they are well aware that there are limitations to any test. As an example, no single test can evaluate a student or students on everything that has been taught and/or learned in a class. The test or assigned project just measures a sample of the possible test questions or possible assigned projects.

Other groups and organizations such as the publishers of *Education Week,* the American Education Research Association, and the American Psychological Association have joined the current voices of protest. This concern is not new, however. Nearly three decades ago, the National Education Association took a very aggressive step based on the misuses and abuses of standardized intelligence tests and other achievement tests and called for a moratorium on such tests. Currently, some organizations, educators, and parents have critiqued testing practices. Alfie Kohn (2000) in *The Case Against Standardized Testing: Raising the Scores, Ruining the Schools* endorses this criticism. He urges that, "No single measure should decide a student's academic fate."

Despite the raised voices and the concerned, often hostile words, high-stakes testing is pervasive. In high-stakes testing, a single test is used to decide whether a student is promoted from one grade to another or is graduated from high school. Such misuse or abuse completely ignores principles of research and statistical findings. It ignores the unanimous opposed voices of main American education organizations which represent major subjects or content areas. It also ignores history.

A very painful chapter in America's history occurred when an intelligence test was administered to immigrants, scored, and then used to label them "feeble-minded." Vito Perrone (1977) in *The Abuses of Standardized Testing* tells how that happened in 1912 when Henry Goddard, an American psychologist, went to Ellis Island and inappropriately administered the Binet Intelligence Test to immigrants as if it were a perfect assessment tool. From this testing, Goddard judged that 83% of Jews, 80% of Hungarians, 79% of Ukrainians, and 87% of Russians were "feeble-minded." This practice not only used the Binet Intelligence Test as if it were a perfect test, but it also ignored the importance of what Chase called the " . . . complex of abilities and experiences . . ." learners " . . . bring to the learning situation." Surely, these immigrants neither had the knowledge of American culture and the English language nor the needed experiences to understand the concepts or tasks presented on the Binet Intelligence Test.

The use of high-stakes tests is certainly as abusive for students who for whatever reason have not had the academic exposure to help them develop the skills and "complex of abilities and experiences" needed for mastering required tests. Such practice is as inappropriate as Goddard's use of the Binet Intelligence Test with immigrants.

COMPLEX OF LEARNING AND EXPERIENCES— PRIOR KNOWLEDGE

Because a test should be an integral part of learning, it is important for the teacher to pretest students at the outset of a new course, new unit, or new learning activity to determine if students possess the needed concepts, knowledge, and experiences which will lead to understanding and meaningful learning. If the needed concepts, knowledge, and experiences are missing, the teacher should help to create them by reviewing the past or basic concepts needed to learn the new concepts, by checking to determine how much of the needed knowledge students possess in a new subject, by reading or re-reading easier material on the particular subject, by providing the students with organizing or predicting experiences, and many other activities. Such an approach helps students experience success in learning.

If Henry Goddard had given the immigrants the intelligence test in their own language on their own cultural experiences, the results would probably have been different. Or, if Goddard had administered the Binet after the immigrants had had time to master the American culture and experiences, the English language, and needed test concepts or tasks, the results would have

been undoubtedly quite different. Not only were the immigrants who were tested in 1912 by Henry Goddard at a disadvantage because they did not know
the language, culture, and needed concepts, but they were subjected to
teacher/tester insensitivity which amounts to test abuse.

The testing or assessment abuse did not stop with the immigrants of
1912. In a recent autobiographical sketch, Edward Nieto (2001), a 22 year old
who has had his writing published in the *San Francisco Examiner's YO' Youth
Outlook* tells his poignant experience in school—kindergarten through community college. His sketch is entitled "School Gave Up on Me Before I Got
There." In this article, Nieto discusses being assessed as a special education student in kindergarten, however, because special education did not begin in the
kindergarten, he was skipped to the first grade. Because of the stigma attached
to special education, he often was verbally pelted with painful labels such as
"special ed and disabled." He was limited to the courses that he was allowed
to take and discouraged from pursuing career paths and skill development that
he knew he would be able to master. The accumulation of negative experiences
influenced Nieto's decision to drop out of community college. After college,
he taught himself computer skills. He is currently a staff writer, and ironically
his first job was that of cashier, a job that his teacher told him that he would
be unable to do.

How sad that a single assessment poisoned this young man's school academic and social experiences, but how wonderful that Edward did not let the
negative school experiences define him. He has continued to educate himself—
he has found and is still finding that it is "real-life" or "authentic" performance
that counts. He taught himself computer skills; he is practicing his writing.
Edward has not and is not letting others' narrow view of assessment limit his
goals. However, Edward's bridge to success could have been a great deal
more secure if his teachers did not believe that assessment is perfect rather than
seeing that it has errors and limitations in it.

Phillip Schlechty (1990), author of *Schools for the Twenty-First Century*, has
a philosophy of testing which bears repeating as it was completely overlooked
in Edward Nieto's experience in school. It is that " . . . reading assessments—
and most other assessments as well—should only be conducted when a teacher,
or group of teachers, indicates a child is capable of doing well on the assessment." Observation of Edward and authentic assessments of his skills through
journals and portfolios might have helped the teachers to see that their assessment of him was not correct.

Grant Wiggins (1999) in *Assessing Student Performance* has also presented an approach to student evaluation that may have helped Edward and could
have discouraged a psychologist like Henry Goddard from misusing tests on

immigrants. Wiggins says that standards should be set for each content area based on performance standards like those of musicians, artists, and athletes. He maintains that the standard itself is an ideal. Students' achievements should be placed on a learning/performance continuum of novice (N) for a beginning level, apprentice (A) for a developmental level, and veteran (V) for the student who has mastered the skill, concept, or project. Wiggins finds that this evaluation to be more helpful when evaluating a student's performance than the current norm-referenced presentation of the results of a test. (The norm-referenced test compares one student's scores with a group of his/her peers.) Wiggins' approach to evaluating learning on a performance continuum is also more helpful than a criterion-referenced test, which compares the student's performance with a preset score. The preset point may be a cut-off point for passing the test, such as 200 points, which may be at or above a preset percentage such as 75% mastery of test material. But the student's criterion-referenced test score usually does not show the student's place on the learning continuum.

The experiences that the immigrants had when Goddard inappropriately administered the Binet Intelligence Test and the experiences of Edward Nieto are common among many poor students, who in America are disproportionately minorities. They often have not had the opportunities to develop the complex of abilities, learning experiences, and prior knowledge—learning links or connections—that prepare them to acquire given skills. Like the immigrants of 1912 and Edward Nieto, they have been labeled and, therefore, not been given opportunities to learn those skills even which they knew they could learn or excel in. Often, there is no attempt to help students like Edward Nieto to develop or create the complex of abilities, experiences, or learning links or connections. The rationalization for failing to help create prior knowledge in such students is that such knowledge should have been acquired at home or at an earlier grade. Without the skills and without the opportunities to acquire complex abilities and crucial skills, students are often held accountable for these abilities and skills in a formal testing situation. These conditions or practices are forms of test abuse. This is exactly what happened to the immigrants that Goddard tested in 1912 and Edward Nieto.

Two other problems have affected students as exemplified in the cases in the state of Illinois in 2003 and those students who were assessed on the National Adult Literacy Survey in 1992. In the December 28, 2003, issue of the *Chicago Tribune* an article entitled "State (Illinois) tosses 80,000 tests— Move inflates achievement scores at nearly 1,400 schools" describes the conditions that led to the disqualification of so many of the 2003 Illinois State Achievement Tests. The tests were disqualified for two reasons: one was that incomplete tests were invalid, and the second one was that the tests of students who had enrolled in an Illinois school on or after October 1, 2002, were disqualified. Failure to comply to the standards were the reason for the invalidation. Both of these standards were based on the changed Illinois rules that were aligned with the advent of federal reforms. It seems that neither the teachers nor the administrators clearly understood the move. Dan Bugler, the Chicago school district's chief of research, said, "There has been a lot of confusion in general, over the report card data, and we are not sure exactly what happened with these test scores." (Rado and others, 2003) And, his statement seems to reflect the opinions of other administrators and teachers. If teachers and administrators are confused about this issue, then other stakeholders—parents, students, and the community—must be totally baffled. An important way to avoid confusion in testing, which is test misuse, is to make sure that the test administration, interpretation, and general rules are understood by all stakeholders.

In another article, the National Adult Literacy Survey of 1992 and other testing and learning issues are examined by Anthony Manzo in the May 2003 issue of the *Journal of Adolescent and Adult Literacy* (Manzo, May 2003). In the article "Literacy Crisis or Cambrian Period? Theory, Practice, and Public Policy Implications," Manzo discusses how the criterion—the preset standard for passing—for the National Adult Literacy Survey in 1992 for determining literacy was set at an 80% accuracy level rather than a 65% accuracy level, the one which the National Assessment of Educational Progress uses. While using the correct criterion level, there was still a literacy problem, but it was not at the crisis level. Whether the error involved uninformed Chicago administrators or a wrong decision by the statisticians in setting the criterion, both cases are examples of test abuse or misuse.

In the case of the criterion-setting error in the Literacy Survey, Manzo determined that the perception of a crisis led many states to develop their own quick-fix criterion-referenced, high-stakes tests. The results of the 1992 report, however, were not re-examined until 2002. It was found that 1992 criterion—passing standard or cutoff—set for the 26,000 adults who were tested on the survey was indeed too high. This is a type of test misuse where the results produced incorrect information about a number of those taking the test. As a reminder, Manzo outlines factors that negatively affect testing results. These are factors that Goddard seemed to overlook. Among the overlooked factors of the immigrants whom he tested are those of possessing little knowledge of the culture of the new country, having limited-English language proficiency, experiencing physical or linguistic problems, and other factors that greatly influence a student's performance. Further, he mentions a number of other things that influence the success of a person such as resilience, application of information to real-life situations, critical thinking, and other tasks not assessed on achievement tests directly but that must be considered in looking at the state of literacy. These factors must be taken into consideration in all achievement testing.

UNIQUENESS OF EACH STUDENT

A common pronouncement in the mission statement of schools is one that vows to honor the uniqueness of each child. Another point that is often made in such statements is that all children can learn. The following anonymous statement, however, should be reflected in the ideals of schools: "If children cannot learn the way we teach them, we must teach them the way they learn." This statement complements any mention of "uniqueness" and the fact that "all children can learn." However, in our current academic climate, these claims ring hollow. Instead of saluting the uniqueness of each child or the idea that all children can learn or finding the optimal way of teaching students, our current practices—especially high-stakes testing—say that all children are the same. It says that all children have had the same experiences, learn at the same pace, and learn in the same way.

Practice or **action** rather than **talk** determines how educators and the public feel about children. If we truly feel that each child is unique, not only will the teaching/learning environment include varied approaches to teaching and learning but multiple-types of assessments as well. What is taught and learned in each class will reflect research and best practices. Among such practices will be collaborative learning and interactive teaching and learning. Students will be exposed to innovative teaching. Multiple modalities—all possible senses—and all of the language arts—reading, writing, listening, and speaking—will be used in order to tap into the uniqueness of students and to spark student interest and motivation in all classroom activities. Even the visual and performing arts will be used to stimulate learning in the content areas.

In tapping the uniqueness of each child or student, teachers should provide opportunities for different types of learning. Some students learn by receptive learning in which the student is basically told or given information by the teacher; this is what occurs in a lecture approach. Some will learn by modeling or observing, for example, watching science experiments or demonstrations or seeing how a teacher or another person performs in certain learning situations. Still other students may learn by discovery learning (heuristics). This is often done in a classroom by what is called "hands-on" activities. It is also the way many inventors, scientists, and artists learn. Some children/ students are convergent thinkers; they come up with one answer. On the other hand, others are divergent thinkers. They may come up with multiple answers for a learning situation. This type of thinking is often called creative thinking. Multiple-choice types of test experiences are favorable to convergent thinkers. Creative thinkers are often penalized in multiple-choice-type questions because they see many answers for the question.

One example of divergent/creative thinking that I experienced recently points this out. In an individual formal testing situation (one student is tested by one test administrator), I witnessed an example of divergent thinking. (Most of the questions on an individual formal test are answered orally. The administrator both sees and hears the student's work on the problems and the production of his/her answers. Because the test is one to one, the test administrator is permitted to ask such questions as, "Do you want to try again?" "Is that all?"). The problem stated that Tim went to bed at 10:30 P.M. He got up at 7:00 A.M. The questions was *How many hours did Tim sleep?* The student being tested, who is undoubtedly a divergent or creative thinker, said that Tim slept 8 hours. The answer key listed the correct answer as 8 1/2 hours." When I asked the student, "Is there anything more?" He said, "Oh, yes, there are 30 minutes or 1/2 hour left but, 30 minutes or 1/2 hour is not an hour. Of course, the student was given credit for his answer. In a sense the student was thinking more exactly than the person who designed the test question. However, in a group test where the student had to write or mark a correct answer, the student would have been penalized for his initial answer. Such an experience shows the importance of anticipating and looking at the uniqueness of learners.

Divergent thinkers may think beyond the answer presented in the textbook, by the teacher, or on a test. Probably most students can learn to some degree by each type of learning approach, but one student may learn better or more effectively by one approach than another. For this reason, learners should be provided with experiences that require different thinking approaches. However, some students may, as a regular mode of operating, use one approach rather than another. Because of this, multiple thinking approaches should be used and encouraged.

In addition to examining the various types of thinking, a thorough investigation of the uniqueness of each child should include both research and/or successful practices if there is a lack of substantial research. Such approaches as preferred learning styles and tactile and kinesthetic approaches should be encouraged in learning, teaching, and testing. Failure to identify and encourage the uniqueness of individuals caused some geniuses, inventors, leaders, and great artists to be incorrectly evaluated. A further consideration is that a number of great leaders, inventors, artists, and geniuses would not have passed today's high-stakes or pervasive proficiency tests.

In the past as well as today, many divergent thinkers were/are misunderstood or misevaluated. Alan Loy McGinnis (1990) in his book *The Power of Optimism* pointed out how many of our past leaders, inventors, geniuses, and artists were often incorrectly evaluated. McGinnis emphasizes this by sharing the following examples that reflect what he saw posted on a college bulletin board:

- When Thomas Edison was seven years old, his teacher described him to an inspector as hopeless, "addled," and wasting his time in attending school.
- While Abraham Lincoln was described as a good student by his teacher after having attended school for only four months, the teacher said that he was a daydreamer and asked foolish questions.
- Woodrow Wilson was described as a unique member of the class. Further, the teacher said he was ten years old and was just beginning to read and write. She cautioned his parents that they must not have high aspirations for him.
- Albert Einstein was described as a very poor student who was mentally slow, a daydreamer, and unsociable. The teacher recommended that he be removed from school since he was spoiling learning for the remainder of the class.
- Amelia Earhart, an American aviator, was described as bright and curious, but the teacher said that she had a strange interest in bugs and other crawling things, and her daredevil projects were not fitting for a young lady.
- Caruso was told by his teacher that he had no voice.
- Louisa May Alcott was told by an editor that she would never "write anything for popular consumption."

The uniqueness of the above students was not recognized by their teachers. These people were probably divergent thinkers. In school, it is often the convergent thinkers who are rewarded. Primarily, this is because the convergent thinkers come up with the answer that the teacher expects. Divergent thinkers, on the other hand, may see multiple answers in classroom or testing experiences. However, teachers must recognize that receptive learning, where the teacher is the teller or the giver of information, is more helpful to convergent thinkers than to divergent thinkers. Heuristic or discovery learning is more helpful to divergent thinkers. To tap the uniqueness of each student in a classroom, multiple approaches that encourage divergent thinking as well as convergent thinking should be used.

The uniqueness of Richard Rhodes was accepted by Yale University when they awarded him a scholarship in 1955. Maybe, it was that they knew that all tests have errors in them or that students cannot be expected to know what they have not been taught. In Richard Rhodes' (1990) autobiography, *A Hole in the World,* he recounts his acceptance by Yale University. He said, "I scored high on the College Board aptitude tests but below average on the achievement tests.

I'd never written an essay in my life. I hadn't read Jack London or Joyce Kilmer or Washington Irving. I still haven't." A Yale representative later told Rhodes, "We knew you were bright, but we weren't sure you were literate." Born during the Depression; he had been deserted by his family—his biological mother committed suicide when he was only thirteen months old; his stepmother, with whom he lived from the time he was ten until he was twelve, was psychologically and physically abusive to him and his older brother; his father was meek and complacent and allowed his sons to be abused. His brother, though, protected him by reporting the beatings and starvation to the police department who placed the boys in Andrew Drumm Institution, a home for boys. At Andrew Drumm, the boys were safe but not academically enriched. Richard was a voracious reader but just books of interest to him. In 1955, he was designated to receive the annual Yale scholarship that was awarded to a boy at Andrew Drumm. Yale's decision was correct. Rhodes graduated from Yale. Today, he is the author of twenty books, among them are his autobiography, his Pulitzer Prize and National Book award winning *The Making of the Atomic Bomb*, and his 2004 publication of *John James Aubudon: The Making of an American.*

Testing experiences, too, must include approaches and experiences that accommodate the uniqueness of each student. It is important to remember that many of our geniuses, leaders, inventors, even some presidents attended schools that did not take into account the uniqueness of these American heroes and heroines.

WEIGHING VARIABLES THAT AFFECT STUDENT LEARNING AND TEST RESULTS

Like student uniqueness, many other crucial variables that greatly affect learning, teaching, and testing are often overlooked or given "lip service." Research shows that student performance is often influenced by conditions and/or variables within as well as conditions and/or variables outside the school. Some of the variables within the school that affect student performance are administrator and teacher preparation, school climate, materials, parent involvement, enriching "real life" experiences, equipment, technology, and funding. Outside-the-school variables that affect student performance include social and economic resources of families, schools, communities, local, state, and federal governments. When looking at the within-school variables as well as the outside-the-school variables that affect student performance, it is necessary for education and sociology to be part of a complementary approach.

Often when talking about the variables that affect America's diverse schools, many lay people as well as educators speak in terms of "leveling the playing field." In the same vein, many educators and researchers would speak of having constants—things that are the same—in as many critical educational and sociological areas affecting the school as possible. This would mean that many important conditions which usually vary in all schools—administrator and teacher preparation, materials, enriching "real life" experiences, equipment, technology, and funding—would be much the same within the community and state as well as throughout the country. On the other hand, researchers would agree that while the outside-the-school variables could be observed, discussed, and evaluated, they cannot be held constant. Even to have variables as constants within the school would be viewed as a benefit but probably an impossibility.

While the variables affecting schools have been neatly divided in this book into within-school variables and outside-the-school variables, in reality, they are indivisible. They are intertwined. For chronology's sake, outside-the-school variables—social and economic resources of families, communities, and local, state, and federal governments—will be looked at first. These variables—especially the family—are the genesis of education. In American families, the social and economic resources and levels vary greatly. However, these levels are not static—they can and do change. Unfortunately, change in this area is not only difficult but slow. These variables are on a continuum from the homeless family who has little or no social and economic independence to the wealthy family who is both socially and economically independent. All families are affected to some degree by current social and economic problems and concerns, but the social and economic problems and concerns disproportionately affect the families who are at the bottom of the social and economic ladder (who are often labeled as disadvantaged) and who are disproportionately minorities.

Looking at the variables in the socioeconomic levels listed here, it should be noted that there are numerous levels in between these three levels. The average level would include the greatest number of families. This category would include factory, blue-collar, and some professional workers who earn middle-level incomes. (A book on sociology will describe these categories more precisely than is being done here.) A consideration of sociology and history is important when looking at the variables that affect students in our nation's schools.

OUTSIDE-THE-SCHOOL-SETTING VARIABLES

Poor families are often dependent on some type of social agency for support or, they may live on their own with very meager funds, services, and resources.

Many of these families are headed by single mothers. Even though the poor do not fit neatly into one category, there is one thing which is generally true of poor families, they live in poor neighborhoods, and their children usually go to poor schools. Further, they generally are not served well by the local, state, or federal governments. In many poor urban areas, local or state governments propose the building or housing of prisons in their neighborhoods. Their environments are often contaminated by toxic pollutants from factories and other sources of toxic waste.

It is easy to know when you are in a poor area of a city without seeing the people because much of the infrastructure is in disrepair. Generally, the houses, apartments, and the few business establishments are dilapidated or poorly maintained. Sanitation services as well as snow removal or street cleaning may happen on a "last served basis." There are few agencies to help with reinforcing or enriching educational experiences for students and families. There is often great local mobility in the poor family; they often move from one poor neighborhood to another and one poor school to another. If you look at the residents of poor areas of the city, many of them have been poorly served by employment agencies, by the social service agencies, by the schools, and by the justice system. Further, many people in poor areas may be unemployed or in some cases underemployed; a number of them may have been incarcerated.

The average and above-average socioeconomic-level families are usually employed, whether this employment is a blue-collar position, a factory job, or a medium- salary professional position. Their homes and businesses, usually modest in cost and size, are well maintained. Their community services are usually at worst mediocre. There are some social agencies in the community that help with reinforcing or enriching educational experiences for students and families. The average and above-average families are often upwardly mobile. They usually want the best for their children and investigate sources and resources that will help in the social and educational development of their children. They often have long-range plans for their children.

The upper-level/wealthy families are usually professional and/or college educated. Some families may be owners of businesses or entrepreneurs. Some families may have inherited money. At any rate, they have an abundance of money, services, and resources. They usually live in immaculate communities and homes. These families may have paid domestic help. They receive excellent services from the local, state, and federal governments. Businesses that line their commercial strips are long established and well maintained. These families want their children to live up to the high standards of their family. Not only do their communities often have organizations that reinforce and enrich the education of students and families, but they also support, collaborate with, and mentor the educational endeavors for youth, colleagues, and/or friends. In addition, travel, exposure to the visual and performing arts, museums, spas, sports events, and many other enriching activities are regular occurrences in their lives. What is more they have the money and usually the time to provide enrichment for every member of their family.

The schools for each socioeconomic level usually reflect the socioeconomic conditions of the communities in which they are housed. As would be expected, schools reflect the problems and operating values of the general society.

WITHIN-SCHOOL VARIABLES

In America, even though there is universal education, in many cases it is separate and unequal. Although this expression is usually thought as indicating a racial divide, probably a more critical demarcation is between the "haves" and "have nots," whether they be urban or rural. Unfortunately, the poor are disproportionately members of minority groups. The poor go to poor schools. While these schools usually have a core of teachers and administrators who are well trained, dedicated, and interested in the students' academic and social growth, they often have a disproportionate number of teachers and administrators who may be still working on certification or licensure and others whose tenure by choice is short lived. Because of the shortage of teachers, many of these schools have substitutes manning classes on a regular basis. They have fewer materials, less technology, less equipment, and a paucity of general resources than schools in more affluent areas. The availability of technology usually lags behind that found in more affluent schools by as much as a decade. When technology is available, the complementary pieces are often unavailable. For example, there may be some computers available without the necessary software. This is true even of the human resources. Few parents volunteer in the schools. In many cases this has to do with the lack of comfort that the parents feel in the school environment.

There are, however, some schools which serve children in poor or working class areas that are stellar. Such schools are often oases in communities where most resources and hope have "dried up." One such school is Suder Elementary school located in the Henry Horner housing project in Chicago, one of nation's worst housing projects. Not only was this school praised by Alex Kotlowitz (1991) in of *There Are No Children Here,* but the school and the principal Brenda Daigre were spotlighted in the September 23, 1991, issue of

Newsweek. (Kantrowitz, 1991) The principal is both a disciple and a maverick, who despite the Third World conditions of the community in which the school is housed, has created a school that is safe, clean and pleasant, academically enriched, and student supportive. Each year Daigre raises funds so that twelve to fifteen Suder students can travel to the continent of Africa. She realizes the value of students knowing the larger world community. Equally as important, she realizes that a well-run school socially and academically can make a difference in the education and lives of students—poor as well as average or wealthy.

Like Suder, most exemplary urban and rural schools which educate the poor are stellar because of dedicated staffs who give countless extra hours of their time and their personal funds to make the schools succeed. Such schools usually do not have funding equal to that of suburban schools with comparable numbers of students. The extra funds usually come from public solicitation such as that which the principal of Suder vigorously pursued. Many schools that serve the poor have little or no funds for enrichment and sometimes very few funds for basic materials such as books, equipment, and supplies. In fact, many states like Ohio have been sued over inequity of funding. In one lawsuit, Ohio lost a State Supreme Court decision because inequitable funding of schools is in violation of the U.S. Constitution. Some of the issues resulting in the lawsuits were discussed in the November 22, 1993, *Cleveland Plain Dealer* article from the Associated Press, entitled "Professor Says Poor Schools Don't Get Fair Share of Funds." The article cited a study by Kern Alexander of Virginia Polytechnic Institute and University. His study found that "Ohio is one of the most poorly equalized states in United States, . . . in 1990–91, the top 20% of the rich school districts received $547 million more in state and local funding than the poorest 20% of school districts," and a comparison of the state average millage is 29.6 mills for rich schools but 26.8 mills for poor districts. Further, he found that teachers in the richest 10% of the school districts had average annual salaries that were over $12,000 more than in the bottom 10% of the school districts, that students in rich school districts had a much greater choice of courses, including opportunities for advanced-placement courses, and that poor school districts served 12.16% of special needs students while rich school districts served 10.7%. ("Professor Says . . . ." 1993, B3)

The infrastructure of the schools that serve the poor is usually similar to the infrastructure of the neighborhoods of the poor—they are both in disrepair. Kozol's (1996) educational video on Ohio schools entitled *Children in America's Schools—Beautiful Flowers Growing in a Garbage Can* documented the fact that some rural schools in the state still had outhouses and that many urban schools are falling down. In Cleveland, Ohio, during the 2000–2001 school year, the ceiling and a wall collapsed in a high school gymnasium. In

January 23, 2001, an article relating to the disaster was printed in the *Plain Dealer,* stating that a civic committee urged the passage of a $380 million bond issue for the Cleveland Public Schools saying, "We have seen firsthand the deplorable conditions which characterize the majority of the district's facilities. . . ." (Townsend and Okoben, 2001, A1)

Many authors have also told of the same deplorable conditions in the schools that serve the poor in America. Most noted among these authors is Jonathan Kozol (1992, 1995, 1996), who has been actively describing poor facilities and lack of academic opportunities in many of our urban schools in such books as *Savage Inequalities, Illiterate America,* and *Amazing Grace.* Lisbeth Schorr (1989), like Kozol, describes the hopeless type of school environments which are causing many of the poor to leave school "unschooled and unskilled" in her book entitled *Within Our Reach.* This disparity is also described by Doris Entwisle and others (1997) in *Children, Schools, & Inequality.* So many authors and sociologists are moved to write about the schools for the poor because they are exact opposites of the model American School.

On the other hand, the schools that serve the middle class, upper middle class, or wealthy are written about sparingly. While these schools are not perfect, their problems are few in number. When academic problems do happen, the school, the family, and the community usually provide supportive services. All schools do have isolated social problems as the shootings at Columbine; Paduca, Kentucky; Santee, California; and other schools poignantly show.

Schools for the middle class and upper class students are part of the focus on general restructuring of all of the nation's schools, the new model for American schools. Education revolves about change. So, with this in mind many theorists and authors have written about suggested changes for the twenty-first century. These authors and theorists have discussed such things as authentic experiences, including testing, active learning, interactive learning, cooperative learning, effective schools as well as constructivist-type learning, and general changes needed in the school. John Goodlad (1984) has discussed many new crucial issues and substantive, needed changes in the study presented in his book *A Place Called School.*

Linda Lambert and others (1995) in *The Constructivist Leader* have discussed the obsolescence of our schools and the need to reinvent them. This is needed to ensure that the school experience is authentic, has interaction as a goal, has experiences and opportunities for an ever-expanding world view, has a wide array of participants—parents, students, teachers, administrators, community people, and more—and attempts to make school a place of growth for all.

Phillip Schlechty (1990), in *Schools for the Twenty-first Century,* talks about his inquiry of corporate leaders as to what they want from the schools. They responded that, "We need people who know how to learn. Knowing how to learn, they seek to learn on purpose, to learn from class, from books, from instructors." Further, it is hoped that they will seek information to solve problems and use others as resources in solving problems. Schlechty and other authors present many other ideas needed as America restructures its schools for the twenty-first century. Their propositions, goals, and objectives are for all students; therefore, if the proposals for restructuring become a reality, the propositions, goals, and objectives will be constants in all schools.

The variables that separate poor students from middle class and upper class students are in such crucial areas that many educators term the poor population at risk. According to Doris Entwisle and others in *Children, Schools, & Inequality,* the support of parents and the general community most greatly affects students in the summer when middle class and wealthy families often travel or explore enriching experiences locally and use the many community resources that support "cognitive growth when the schools are closed." Such experiences are not available to the poor. [Based on fall test scores, poor students' scores decline over the summer while scores of students in a high socioeconomic level increase over the summer.] These variables are not new to researchers and theorists. Entwisle and others found that, " . . . the developmental level of all children needs to be brought up to that of better-off children by the time they start first grade, and *we know how to do this.*" The remarks of the authors of *Children, Schools, & Inequality* seem to mirror those of Lisbeth Schorr in *Within Our Reach* when she says as Americans we have it within our reach to change the rotten outcomes of students who leave school unschooled and unskilled; America just has to develop the will to do this.

The variables presented a number of times in this section constitute areas that critically influence a student's success or failure in school. In fact, James McPartland and Robert Slavin in their 1990 policy perspective entitled *Increasing Achievement of At-Risk Students At Each Grade Level Series: Policy Perspectives* present four variable that are predictors of having a near zero chance of graduating from high school: (1) reading one school year below grade level; (2) having been retained in a grade; (3) having a low-socioeconomic background; and (4) attending school with many other poor children. In statistics, such difference would be considered significant. Further, this difference is often so great that statisticians or researchers would say that the poor when compared with the other socioeconomic levels constitute a different population. Therefore, academic comparisons are usually unfair.

The U.S. Kerner Commission (1968) almost four decades ago stated that "Our nation is moving toward two societies, one black and one white—separate and unequal." In 2005 and years to come, these societal divisions are and will be between the poor, the middle class, and the rich more so than just black and white. But even now, the fact that the poor are disproportionately minorities makes Kerner's statement generally true today.

As far as the current trend in "high-stakes" testing, this socioeconomic difference is often disregarded as far as comparison of performance. While most general achievement tests do compare the performance of students with other students of comparable age or grade levels (norm-referenced tests), performance on many of the state proficiency-type tests is evaluated based on a predetermined achievement level. Such comparison is called criterion referenced. Even though the individual tests are compared to a criterion or preset standard, the sum of the results is compared by grade level district to district. This comparison, in a sense, makes the proficiency test norm referenced. This comparison is usually done in what is called the "report card," which often appears in local newspapers.

Such widely publicized comparison of test performance data is professionally wrong and a misuse of test information. Even in a casual discussion of test performance of these socioeconomic levels, there should be a warning or caveat that states that the conditions among these groups are not comparable based on the significant difference of the conditions under which the low socioeconomic level students have been living both within the school and outside the school setting. Alfie Kohn (2000) in *The Case Against Standardized Testing* says the publicizing of test data creates winners and losers, and if such information has to be publicized, it should be at least put in the right newspaper section—Sports section. Kohn has said knowing how much a mother earns is a good variable for predicting a student's success on such test.

The results of batteries of achievement tests, just like batteries of medical test results, should be accompanied by a prescription or suggested intervention. The intervention should provide teaching/learning strategies for those who scored below average as well as providing enrichment or developmental teaching/learning strategies for those who score average or above average. Just as in medicine, the prescription should be preventive as well as curative.

How can America make sure that the same conditions for learning exist within each school as far as materials; technology; equipment; well-trained, dedicated teachers; equity in funding; and safe, pleasant work conditions? It is imperative to carry out the ideals incorporated in a number of overused ideas that seldom become realities and to make them part of the fabric of every school. These ideas are "All children can learn," "Leave no child behind," and "Level the playing field." Lizbeth Schorr (1989) in *Within Our Reach* and Doris Entwisle, Karl Alexander, and Linda Olson (1997) in *Children, Schools,*

& Inequality state that we—Americans—know how to do this. But, as Schorr states, what America must do now is develop the **will.**

Developing the will would certainly mean that we must be guided by the message in the words of Clinton Chase, "The extent to which children (learners) can acquire a given skill depends on the complex of abilities and experiences they bring to the learning situation." If and when America understands the wisdom in this statement instead of trying to find the perfect test—a misuse of test results—to make critical education and life decisions, educators will begin using an array of assessments. These assessments will range from very informal to formal and will evaluate social as well as academic development in order to get as holistic a picture as possible so that each student can be started at the appropriate social and academic levels and continue on his/her educational journey to mastery academically and socially. This approach will not only change education in America but the complexion of our society where our current practices in teaching and learning, inclusive of testing, are in conflict with research, best practices, educational philosophies, mission statements, educational wisdom, and America's professed values.

USING RESEARCH FINDINGS, SOCIOLOGY, AND HISTORY TO GUIDE TEST PRACTICES

Like the last section, research findings, sociology, and history are important areas to investigate in all aspects of education. Since the information is readily available, the fact that they are taught and examined in isolated college classes but not integrated into the classroom as vital information for teaching and learning is problematic to teachers and students. Knowledge from such areas should be used to understand what, why, when, and how to teach, monitor, and evaluate learning. Such areas of omission are forms of academic abuse, especially because research findings provide many answers to educational problems in teaching, learning, and testing. It is important to understand how all of a student's social environment affects his/her academic performance and how history leaves its mark on all students.

USING RESEARCH FINDINGS

Many authors and researchers have discussed vital research findings on the variables within and outside the school setting that affect teaching and learning and test performance. As in medicine, the stakeholders in education must be aware of research and insist on its implementation, of the application of best practices, of the availability of technology, of the recognition of the uniqueness of each student, of the appropriate use of formal and informal testing, and of all the other factors that affect learning and teaching. With such focus, education, including current learning, teaching, and testing can be positively changed in America. Stakeholders will know that "If children cannot learn the way we teach them, we must teach them the way they learn." In such a climate, tests—self assessment, observation, authentic, real life, informal, and formal—will be integral, ongoing, supportive parts of teaching and learning. Students will realize that learning is on a continuum and that they, therefore, must be lifelong learners. They will leave school knowing their place on the learning continuum in each content area, not with what Lisbeth Schorr (1989) calls "rotten outcomes" or leaving school "unschooled and unskilled."

Yet, there is often no marriage between research and current classroom practices, little awareness and/or implementation of current research, nor the other factors that would place each student on his/her optimal learning continuum. The following research-based, best-practices-based strategies and classroom approaches should be reflected in teaching, learning, and testing— formal, informal, and authentic:

- Active, participatory, integrated, student-centered learning is more effective than passive, teacher-centered learning. (Yet, Goodlad in 1984 found that the majority of 1000 classrooms which he observed were models of the passive learning, teacher-centered approach.)
- Early and ongoing, substantive, clarifying, individualized intervention should be part of every school's program.
- Collaborative and cooperative learning is needed since such practices provide students with opportunities to share and weigh the ideas of others. Further, the two approaches represent those used in the "real" world.
- Reading, writing, discussing, and higher-order thinking should be part of learning in all content areas.
- Prior knowledge should be developed for each learning activity.
- Learning is strategic.
- Independent learning is a desired outcome in each content area.
- Culture is reflected in most learning, and multicultural education should be part of every classroom.
- Multiple tools should be used to integrate and to expand student learning. They should include such things as textbooks, newspapers, supplementary materials, trade books, out-of-grade books such as picture books. Computers should be used at all levels and in all content areas.
- Assessment should be ongoing and include many samples of student behavior acquired through formal, informal, and authentic assessments in formative (during the instruction time) and summative (at the end) ways. Creative projects should be part of the assessment program.

The above are just a sample of classroom strategies and approaches that reflect research and best practices. Some key phrases from those listed above are: active learning which is student-centered, culture-centered; uses multiple materials and tools, including computers; ongoing assessments, and utilizes formal, informal, authentic assessments; and creative projects. Failure to use best practices would be like a doctor treating cancer or some other life-threatening disease with untested approaches of four decades ago when current research-tested approaches are available.

SOCIOLOGY

In the beginning chapters of this book, the need was stressed for collaboration among different professionals in the testing process—test designers, test administrators, test evaluators. This same type of collaboration is needed among the stakeholders in the educational development process of the students. Collaboration is the sharing of knowledge. Such sharing would help the teacher to be aware of the student's social environment—family, friends, neighborhood, and church—as well as having the benefits of interaction among stakeholders. This also would be focusing on a factor that all education organizations stress as important: that is, the effect of culture on student learning. Educators must know the students' academic and social environments.

Research has found that the culture of a student greatly affects his/her learning. This is stressed by Faye Steuer (1994) in *The Psychological Development of Children* and by many other books and studies. Knowledge of the student's social environment will give the teacher vital information about the parent's views of education. It will answer such questions as: Does the parent believe that education is a joint or collaborative venture among the home, school, and community? If this is the view of the parent, has he/she exposed the child to reading experiences or even taught the child to read long before he/she becomes a student in a formal classroom? Are there school-type, enriching experiences provided in the local community or through travel? Or, is the parent's view one which shows that he/she incorrectly believes that formal education is the sole domain of the school?

Varied parent and student views are to be expected in the diverse classroom. But it is the teacher who has to develop or have a repertoire of strategies, techniques, and/or approaches not only to begin instruction at the level where the student is but to respect, honor, and nurture the student's culture. If the parent views education as the sole responsibility of the school, not only does the teacher often need to have intervention strategies but may have to ask for support from the learning or intervention specialist in his/her school. (A great deal more information can be explored in this area by reading a book or article on psychological development of the child or a book or article on sociology.)

When educators say that each student is unique and that they respect diversity but teach and test as if each student brings the same prior knowledge to a learning experience, as if each student has the same culture, and as if one type of test or one approach to teaching fits all students, this is a form of academic and/or test abuse.

HISTORY

Historical practices have resulted in less than equal opportunity for many of America's impoverished students. A disproportionate number of the poor are minorities. Often the schools label the students who are poor as disadvantaged or at risk. However, other concerned citizens often talk about the following needs when it comes to the disadvantaged or at risk: level playing fields, equal access, equal opportunity, equity in funding, commitment, change in budgetary priorities and public policies, and many others.

A glimpse into the history of American education reveals that if today's labels of disadvantaged or at risk had been in use before the middle of the twentieth century, there would have been an abundance of students who would have fallen into this category. This is because access to education was then very uneven for middle-class and poor and young women. Until the 1870s when public schools were established, schooling usually occurred at home and through private and church schools. Not very many school-age children attended schools at that time. According to Eric Foner and John Garraty (1991) in *The Reader's Companion to American History*, only 4 percent of children from fourteen to seventeen years of age attended school in 1890. The attendance of school-age children increased greatly in America during the early part of the twentieth century. Two occurrences substantially increased the number of children in school: the passage of the laws for compulsory school attendance in 1918 and the establishment of limits on child labor in 1938.

Even with the new laws, unequal education was/is the rule rather than the exception in America. Foner and Garraty state that as early as the late nineteenth century some religious groups had established schools specifically for Native Americans, poor whites, and blacks. While this was a valiant deed, few were served. At the close of the Civil War only about 5 percent of the former slaves were literate; many of those were self taught. Probably, the religious groups that established the schools for Native Americans, poor whites, and blacks wanted to provide equal access. However, equal access and a level playing field have been distant goals for these three groups. During slavery, education was forbidden for slaves. The 1896 adoption *Plessy v. Ferguson* enforced social segregation in accommodations, including the schools, so that separate but equal became the law of the land. For schools, this practice was legally overturned in 1954 by *Brown v. Board of Education of Topeka*. The Supreme Court unanimously decided that the practices legalized by *Plessy v. Ferguson* produced "separate educational facilities that were 'inherently unequal' because the intangible inequalities of segregation deprived blacks of equal protection under law."

Even though the *de jure* segregation—segregation by law—ended by the 1954 ruling, this did not guarantee equal access as the numerous *de facto* segregation—segregation in fact—lawsuits in the 1970s, 1980s and 1990s proved. Further, the current cry for equal access as well as equity in funding say that American schools for the poor and minorities do not provide the opportunities envisioned in the 1954 decision. So, the inequality that Entwisle and others describe in the schools and neighborhoods seriously affects the education of poor and minority students. In the generation and one-half that have elapsed since the *Brown v. Board of Education of Topeka,* it has become clear that equality in education, especially for the poor and minorities, is still an unsolved problem in America.

Lack of equal opportunity or equal access was observed by John Goodlad (1984) and reported in *A Place Called School.* As a part of a study, Goodlad observed over 1,000 classrooms. He observed that among multiracial schools employing tracking, poor and minority students were found in disproportionally large percentages in the low-track classes, and whites were found in disproportionately large percentages in the high-track classes. As might be expected, the low-track classes were found to be less satisfactory in crucial academic ways than the high-track classes which were said to provide more satisfactory teaching and learning conditions.

How does this inequality affect standardized test scores and other school learning in general? First and foremost, in any district-by-district reporting of scores, anyone can predict which schools will be at bottom of the range of district-by-district results. Predictably, it will be the districts that serve a majority of poor and minority students. Alfie Kohn (2000), in *The Case Against Standardized Testing, Prospects for the Future,* says that a person can predict failure or success of a student by knowing the socioeconomic status of the student's mother.

Ironically, the poor, inclusive of minorities, may have parents and grandparents who feel that they were failed by the schools as students themselves. These parents usually know that neither the neighborhoods nor their schools are academically enriched—poor students live in poor, impoverished neighbors and attend poorly equipped schools. Further, the culture of minorities is not proportionately depicted in the books they use; in many of the texts, minorities and their contributions are usually ignored, unknown, disrespected, or stereotyped. Yet, best practices stress the importance of knowing or tapping into the culture of students. Tests should reflect best learning and teaching practices such as having some assessments that tap into the culture of the student, but often they do not. Tests should only be used if appropriate interventions and/or remediation are going to be available to the student, which, again, is often not the case currently.

ROLES OF LEGISLATORS

Legislators certainly should strive to make the precept " . . . with justice and liberty for all. . . ." a reality by providing equal protection under law, equal access, equal opportunity, and equity in funding for American students. This is the view of the International Reading Association Board (2000) in its position statement entitled *Making a Difference Means Making It Different: Honoring Children's Rights to Excellent Reading Instruction.* Implicit in the ten statements that follow is the concept that legislators' decisions should be made in collaboration with educators who are knowledgeable about assessment and best practices rather than purely for economic or political reasons. Many of the statements involve reading, which is quite logical since the statements are from an organization whose focus is reading and because reading is at the core of almost all learning. Many of the statements involve assessment.

- Children have a right to appropriate early reading instruction based on their individual needs;
- Children have a right to reading instruction that builds both the skill and the desire to read increasingly complex materials;
- Children have a right to access a wide variety of books and other reading materials in classroom, school, and community libraries;

Legislators should:

- Understand that it is not their job to prescribe a particular reading method;
- Provide resources, particularly for schools and children in high-poverty settings, that allow school districts to provide ongoing professional development in reading instructions for teachers and reading specialists and that enable them to provide appropriate reading materials;
- Support further research on successful practice, derived from a range of perspectives;

- Be certain to *not* impose one-size-fits-all mandates;
- Not attempt to manipulate instruction through assessments. In other words, do not initiate, design, or implement high stakes tests when the primary goal is to affect instructional practices;
- Lobby for the development of classroom-based forms of assessment that provide useful, understandable information, improve instruction, and help children become better readers;
- Give attention and appropriate funding for reading and writing services in the upper grades as well as in the early grades.

The quotations from the International Reading Association's position statement support much that has been presented in this chapter, and explicitly state that legislators' major responsibilities are to collaborate with educators as well as observe classroom instruction so that they are aware of classroom as well as cultural needs. Their function should not be to design or mandate one-size-fits-all, high-stakes tests.

REOCCURRING CONCEPTS AND IMPLICATIONS

When in 1912 Goddard administered, scored, interpreted, and used the results of intelligence tests—a form of achievement test—to label immigrants as "feeble minded," he overlooked the advise of Clinton Chase, as quoted previously. While no single test should be used to make major decisions, Goddard's use of intelligence tests was particularly inappropriate, harmful, and abusive. Clearly, a better assessment would have been the use of some authentic assessment of how an immigrant could perform his/her non-language or non-culturally dependent trade, skill, or profession.

Additionally, a one-size-fits-all test would not have in the past nor currently been able to tap the uniqueness of such a genius as Albert Einstein, according to Alan McGinnis (1990) in the *Power of Optimism*. Similarly, Woodrow Wilson at the age of ten would not have done well on any standardized test, nor would he have passed the often-used fourth-grade proficiency test. Certainly, based on the limited view of his teacher, she/he would not have expected that he would grow up to be the president of the United States. Not tapping the uniqueness of each student in various ways through educational programs and formal and informal testing is not only a failure of the school but abusive.

Anthony Manzo (2003) in "Literacy Crisis or Cambrian Period? Theory, Practice, and Public Policy Implications" in the May 2003 issue of the *Journal of Adolescent and Adult Literacy* discusses use of an incorrect criterion on the criterion-referenced National Adult Literacy Survey and how this negatively affected the students who took the tests. Many of the other issues that Manzo presents are aligned with Clinton Chase's convictions. Further, Manzo sees resilience, critical thinking, application of knowledge to real life, and other factors as being clearly reflective of literacy and achievement. (Manzo, 2003)

It must be remembered that the urban poor are disproportionately minorities. Entwisle, Alexander, and Olson in *Children, Schools, & Inequality* stress the importance of enriched academically oriented communities which support the academic growth and development of the schools. This support is not found in communities of the poor. Poor children live in poor homes found in poor communities and languish in poor schools. Failure to consider the reality of the plight of most of the nation's poor is a form of abuse by commission; failure to practice the wisdom found in Chase's works is abuse by omission. *De jure* and *de facto* segregation affected African Americans during most of the twentieth century. *De facto* segregation still affects many minorities in the twenty-first century. Lee Bollinger, president of Columbia University, wrote in *Newsweek* in 2003 that, "Race has been a defining element of the American experience." (Bollinger, January 22, 2003)

Finally, legislators should follow the recommendations of the well-respected education organizations and "not prescribe reading methods or impose other one-size-fits-all mandates." Legislators should work with the leading education organizations to understand many of the complexities of learning, relevant research, changes, and challenges to schools and then try to support the schools through equitable funding, equitable access to education, and equal opportunities in all of the nation's schools. Legislators must practice collaboration among key stakeholders—educators, sociologists, historians, medical people, economists, educational think tanks—to create optimal learning environments for all students. It is an unfair, abusive practice—a misuse of test results—to continue in the direction of having a standardized test reign supreme over research and best educational practices to the detriment of students—especially the poor.

REFERENCES

Bollinger, L. C. (January 27, 2003). "Diversity Is Essential . . ." *Newsweek* 151(4): 32.

Brown v. Topeka Board of Education, Kansas, Shawnee County. (1954). 374 U.S. 483.

Chase, C. I. (1974). *Measurement for Education.* Reading, MA: Addison- Wesley Publishing.

Entwisle, D. R.; Alexander, K. L.; Olson, L. S. (1997). *Children, Schools, & Inequality.* Boulder. CO: Westview.

Foner, E. and Garraty, J. A. (1991). *The Reader's Companion to American History.* Boston: Houghton Mifflin.

Gardner, H. (1983). *Frames of Mind.* New York: Basic Books

Gardner, H. (1991) "Moving Toward More Powerful Assessment." In Perrone, V. (ed.) *Expanding Student Assessment.* Alexandria, VA: Association for Supervision and Curriculum Development, 164–166.

Goodlad, J. (1984). *A Place Called School.* New York: McGraw-Hill.

International Reading Association Board. (2000). (Position Statement). *Making a Difference Means Making It Different: Honoring Children's Rights to Excellent in Reading Instruction.* Newark, DE: International Reading Association.

Kantrowitz, B. (September 23, 1991). "A Is for Ashanti, B Is for Black . . . And C Is for Curriculum Which Is Starting to Change." *Newsweek,* 45–46.

Kohn, A. (2000). *The Case Against Standardized Testing, Prospects for the Future.* Portsmouth, NH: Heinemann.

Kotlowitz, A. (1991). *There Are No Children Here.* New York: Anchor Books, Doubleday.

Kozol, J. (1995). *Amazing Grace.* New York: Crown.

Kozol, J. (1996). *Children in America's Schools: Beautiful Flowers Growing in a Garbage Can.* (Video narrated by Bill Moyers, based on Kozol's book *Savage Inequalities* about Ohio Schools). Columbia, SC: ETV.

Kozol, J. (1992). *Savage Inequalities, Children in America's Schools.* New York: Harper Perennial.

Kozol, J. (2000). *Ordinary Resurrections: Children in the Years of Hope.* New York: Crown.

Lambert, L.; Walker, D.; Zimmerman, D. P.; Cooper, J. E.; Lambert, M. D., Gardner, M. E.; Ford Slack, P. J. (1995). *The Constructivist Leader.* Teachers College, Columbia University. New York: Teachers College Press.

Manzo, A.V. (May 2003) "Literacy Crisis or Cambrian Period? Theory, Practice, and Public Policy Implications." *Journal of Adolescent and Adult Literacy,* 46(2): 854.

McGinnis, A. L. (1990). *The Power of Optimism.* New York: Harper & Row Publishers.

McPartland, J. M. and Slavin, R. E. (1990). *Policy Perspectives: Increasing Achievement of At-Risk Students at Each Grade Level Series: Policy Perspectives.* Washington, D.C.: U. S. Department of Education.

Nieto, E. (January 3, 2001). Editorial: "School Gave Up on Me Before I Got There." San Francisco: *San Francisco Examiner YO' Youth Outlook* NCMonline.com (Pacific News Service), p. B9.

Perrone, V. (1977). *The Abuses of Standardized Testing.* Bloomington, IN: The Phi Delta Kappa Educational Foundation.

Perrone, V. (1991). "Moving Toward More Powerful Assessment." In Perrone. V. (ed.). *Expanding Student Assessment.* Alexandria, VA: Association for Supervision and Curriculum Development.

Plessy v. Ferguson (1896). 163 U.S. 537.

"Professor Says Poor Schools Don't Get Fair Share of Funds." November 22, 1993. *Plain Dealer.* Cleveland, OH, B3.

Rado, D.; Banchero, S.; Little, D. (December 28, 2003). "State Tosses 80,000 Tests—Move Inflates Achievement Scores at Nearly 1,400 Schools." *Chicago Tribune,* A1.

Rhodes, R. (1990). *A Hole in the World: An American Boyhood.* New York: Simon and Schuster.

Schlechty, P. C. (1990). *Schools for the Twenty-first Century: Leadership Imperatives for Educational Reform.* San Francisco: Jossey-Bass.

Schorr, L. B. with Schorr, D. (1989). *Within Our Reach: Breaking the Cycle of Disadvantage.* New York: Anchor Books, Doubleday.

Schreiner, R. (1979). *Reading Tests and Teachers: A Practical Guide.* Newark, DE: International Reading Association.

Steuer, F. B. (1994). *The Psychological Development of Children*. Pacific Grove, CA: Brooks/Cole.

Townsend, A. and Okoben, J. (January 23, 2001)." $380 Million Bond Issue Urged for Cleveland Schools." Cleveland, OH: Plain Dealer.

U.S. Kerner Commission Report, (1968). *Report of the Studies for National Advisory Commission on Civil Disorders*. Washington, DC: U.S. Printing Office.

Wiggins, G. P. (1999). *Assessing Student Performance: Exploring the Purpose and Limits of Testing*. San Francisco: Jossey-Bass.

CHAPTER EIGHT

Accepting Achievement Tests As a Way of Life

> . . . because measuring school effectiveness is extremely complex, it is important that assessment and evaluation focus on more than achievement test results
>
> ROBERT BARR AND WILLIAM PARRETT

Before concluding our brief travels into the area of achievement testing, it is appropriate to revisit the ground which has been covered in this book, including the history of achievement tests as well as the history our country; the positives and negatives of achievement testing; the opinion of stakeholders on achievement testing; the often-overlooked variables in achievement testing such as socioeconomics, uniqueness of learners, limitations of all test instruments, and others. Finally, conditional statements will be made on the use of achievement testing.

It should be remembered that as schools changed at the end of the nineteenth century and the early twentieth century, there was a gradual move in testing from total dependence on the teacher-made subjective test and other informal tests such as spelling and arithmetic tests as tools to measure achievement to the newly developed objective tests. What we now know as the standardized validated achievement test began to blossom with the changing educational needs of our schools.

A glimpse backward would show that by 1900, there was an influx of students into American schools; this continued throughout the twentieth centu-ry. To add to the increased number of students, the incoming school popula-tion grew more diverse. In 1918 compulsory education finally became law for America's school-age children. These changes forced schools to seek achieve-ment testing that would be objective and accommodate the needs of the new population as America focused on educating all students.

In this new educational climate, assessment needs broadened. No longer was a single teacher in charge of all decision making. Curriculum inclusive of achievement testing changed to better serve the growth and diversity of the new school population. The new population required expanded assessment tools. The objective test filled many of the testing demands. At this time, the latter part of the nineteenth century, the shallow roots of what would become very deep-seated roots for the objective standardized test began to grow. Today, it is virtually impossible to find American schoolchildren who have not been exposed to this type of test. With the increase in the number and diversity of students in the 1900s, this type of achievement test became very attractive because of its ease of scoring, saving of teacher time, objectivity, and compa-rability. This comparability allowed the results of a student's performance at one time to be measured against his/her performance at a later time or with groups of the student's age or grade peers.

History shows that, as with any new invention or discovery, the new objective test with all its attractiveness was not a panacea—it was far from per-fect. Today, with all of its revisions, the standardized validated objective test is still not perfect. This is the reason that Robert Barr and William Parrett (1995) in *Hope at Last for At-Risk Youth* have stated that schools should use more than achievement tests to measure school effectiveness. Whether it is school effectiveness or student proficiency that is being assessed, it is impera-tive to use more than a single assessment to make major decisions. When researchers evaluate any test, they do so in light of the facts that there are errors in all measurement and limitations to any test as well as all research. No mea-surement is totally reliable. Even though the standardized objective test has been around for over 100 years, Anne Anastasi points out that it is young in the area of psychological testing. It is still forming and evolving.

HISTORY SHOWS THE FORMATIVE, EVOLVING NATURE OF ACHIEVEMENT TESTING

Much of what is currently needed in the area of achievement testing and what will be needed in the future have roots in some of the past and present knowledge and practices. However, one can expect that there will be revisions, additions, and deletions as well as revisiting and reinstituting of items, concepts, and approaches as our knowledge of achievement testing grows and changes. This will happen because the entire nature of achievement testing is evolving and in a continuous state of growth. Therefore, there will always be a need to study and review current and past research findings and practices.

Such study and review of research and practice have resulted in changes in both informal and formal achievement tests. For example, today when informal assessments require an essay or a short-answer response, the item is often accompanied by a rubric which lets the writer know how different types of responses will be graded. In addition, a checklist is often provided to remind the student to review and revise his/her writing if needed. In the informal use of the essay or essay-type question, the teacher is encouraged to review the writing process with the students. Best practices advocate teaching the writing process and providing students with ongoing practice on the process. This is often done for formal tests on which students are required to provide an essay or an essay-type answer. In the use of the essay in informal assessment, the teacher usually reviews the writing process and includes both a rubric and a checklist to help make what was once a very subjective evaluation fairly objective. This is also true when the checklist and rubric are included for the formal assessment.

Somewhere along the research trail of developing the objective test, the validation process was instituted for tests that were to be used by large segments of the population. This gave some assurance that tests were valid in a number of ways (as discussed in Chapter three) but especially as far as content validity, which relates to a test measuring what the test designer says it does. For example, a reading test that actually measures reading skills and/or tasks is valid. In addition to validity, the new tests were also checked for reliability, clarity, objectivity, possible bias, and stereotypes. To further ensure the fairness and objectivity of the standardized validated test, the test is/was administered and then reviewed with the student population for whom the test was intended in one or two pilot studies prior to using the test as an assessment tool in cases where the results would be placed on the student's record.

The pilot studies were done to correct or revise items where the language was ambiguous or vague or where the concepts were found to be inappropriate by the students in the pilot study. However, even with this safeguard, Oscar Buros (1938) found that many tests which were designed to be administered to large segments of the population had not been validated. Because he was dismayed with the omission of such a crucial part of standardized tests, in 1938, he developed the *Mental Measurement Yearbook*. Buros' original goals and objectives were:

- To provide information about tests published as separates throughout the English-speaking world;
- To present frankly critical test reviews written by testing and subject specialists representing various viewpoints;
- To provide extensive bibliographies of verified references on construction, use, and validity of specific tests;
- To impel test authors and publishers to publish better tests and to provide test users with detailed information on the validation and limitations of their tests;
- To make readily available the critical portions of test reviews appearing in professional journals;
- To suggest to test users better methods of appraising tests in light of their own particular needs;
- To stimulate contributing reviewers to reconsider and think through more carefully their own beliefs and values relevant to testing;
- To present fairly exhaustive listings of new and revised books on testing;
- To inculcate test users with a keener awareness of both the values and limitations of standardized tests; and
- To impress the test users with the need to suspect all tests unaccompanied by detailed data on construction, validity, uses, and limitations—even when products of distinguished authors and reputable publishers.

While the *Mental Measurement Yearbook* is still available, in 1983 Daniel Keyser and Richard Sweetland (1983) developed similar volumes to review and critique newly developed and revised tests. These volumes are called *Test Critiques*. The addition of new test evaluation volumes shows the need for ongoing assessment of new and revised tests to ensure the validity and reliability of widely used tests.

In today's technological revolution, it is possible for teachers as well as parents to request to have access to the validation information from test developers and also to verify this information by using either the *Mental Measurement Yearbook* or *Test Critiques*.

A BRIEF REVIEW OF AMERICAN HISTORY AS IT RELATES TO EDUCATION

At the end of the nineteenth century and beginning of the twentieth century, changes were made in curriculum and testing in order to accommodate the larger and more diverse population. High schools changed their major focus of preparing the elite for college in the college preparatory high school to teaching large numbers of diverse students in the comprehensive high school.

Other issues that affected the schools were related to the climate of the country after the abolition of slavery. This climate arose from the question as to whether to integrate the newly freed blacks into general society inclusive of the schools. This was decided in the negative in the U.S. Supreme Court by *Plessy v. Ferguson* in 1896. A separate but equal decision for all public accommodations including schools became the law of the land and was in effect until 1954. In this year the U.S. Supreme Court decided in *Brown v. Board of Education of Topeka* that "separate educational facilities" were "inherently unequal" because the "intangible inequalities deprived black students of equal protection under the law."

While *de jure* segregation was changed by *Brown v. Board of Education of Topeka,* it did not stop *de facto* segregation. Evidence that desegregation did not work perfectly is found in the lawsuits against segregated school systems of the 1970s, 1980s, and 1990s.

Another factor that remains is the achievement gap. In the Special Report of *U.S. News & World Report*—"50 Years After Brown"—March 22–29, 2004, says of the decision and the expectations, "Yet America still struggles with educating all of its children regardless of the color of their skin." " . . . Fifty years later, that change is unfinished." Under the same topic in "Making History," Justin Ewers (2004) points out that few disagree with the decision of Brown. Even one of the most conservative judges Robert Bork calls Brown "the greatest case in the twentieth century." And, Julian Barnes (March 22–29, 2004) presents data that trace the achievement gap from kindergarten to college. Barnes graphs data from the National Assessment of Educational Progress that show this gap between whites, blacks, and Hispanics, in that order, at the fourth-grade level and at the age of seventeen. Further, he states that while whites and blacks enter college at similar rates, 36 percent of whites graduate with a four-year degree but only 18 percent of blacks. Jobless rates are higher for blacks than whites; incomes are lower for blacks.

Eric Foner and John Garraty (1991), authors of *The Reader's Companion to American History*, state that, "The African-American freedom struggle nevertheless left a permanent mark on American society. Overt forms of racial discrimination and government-supported segregation of public facilities came to an end, although de facto, as opposed to de jure, segregation persisted in northern as well as southern public schools and in other areas of American society."

Lynching, unfair loss of property, race riots, lack of equal opportunity, and the fight for school desegregation certainly have taken a toll on both African American adults and the children who were part of these conflicts and wars. Native Americans and Hispanics have also had a less-than-stellar history in America and American schools as far as experiencing equal opportunity and avoiding violence. While the poor in general have not been subjected to the same overt violence as have African Americans, they still have suffered from lack of equal opportunities. The irony of this is that many minorities belong to racially discriminated groups as well as the socioeconomically discriminated poor groups. The horrendous struggles that many minorities have experienced have had grave effects on their school experiences. This history must be factored in when the fair development and use of achievement tests are considered.

THE POSITIVE AND NEGATIVE EFFECTS OF ACHIEVEMENT TESTING

Achievement testing certainly is an integral part of all learning experiences. As with any test and many products, it is the use, misuse, or abuse that separates the positive from the negative. As an example, a simple product such as toothpaste is used broadly and prescribed by dentists to preserve our teeth. But if you read the label of your tube of toothpaste, you will realize it has negative side effects. There are warnings on all tubes of toothpaste that read: "*Keep out of the reach of children under 6 years of age.* If you accidentally swallow more than used for brushing, seek professional help or contact the poison control center immediately." Unfortunately, there is no such warning on tests, and even these warnings on toothpaste often go unnoticed by the average person.

There are many positive purposes and uses of achievement testing. Formal, informal, and authentic achievement tests can and should be used to get a holistic picture of a student's performance. The idea behind this is that any one achievement test is just a sample of a student's achievement. It takes many different types of samples to get a clear view of a student's achievement. There is an important consideration in the use of multiple assessments, and that is that different people learn and test in unique ways. Another consideration is that it is important to see both the process of learning as well as the product. As an example, watching how a student develops a composition or hearing how a student reads a selection is looking at the process. (The process allows the teacher or evaluator to see how the student writes or reads or approaches mathematics or any other subject. It is the place where the student can be retaught or where intervention can take place if either is needed.) Looking at the completed composition or the completed test answer is looking at a product.

One of the tests to be considered in the holistic use of achievement assessments is the formal test. It is the formal test which is, according to Anne Anastasi (1976), a new instrument in the area of testing. It is also the one which the public hears about most often as educators, legislators, and the general public talk about student's performance on the California Achievement Test

(CAT), the Scholastic Aptitude Test (SAT), or any of the numerous state proficiency tests. The formal assessments usually compare a student's performance with that of other students in that student's age or grade category, or the formal assessment may compare the student's test results with a preset standard or criterion. The positive features of formal tests are numerous. The formal test has been tested for reliability, validity, and objectivity. These tests are economical because a number of students may be tested at one time with a limited number of proctors and administrators; they may be easily scored by the use of a grid or by machine; they are objective—there is a single correct answer. They allow a single student's or a class of students' scores to be compared with other students of the same age or grade in the district, in the state, and in the nation. These features in and of themselves are positive.

The negative features of the formal, informal, or authentic test are many. Informal tests such as teacher-made tests and authentic tests such as projects may reflect a very narrow sample of assessment of what has been taught and expected to be learned, and they may be graded subjectively. They do not allow for broad comparability. An answer that is ambiguous may be scored differently by individual teachers or test administrators. A single teacher's scoring on a project may be challenged by other teachers. Since most projects are in a sense "home grown," their major use is in individual class settings. The formal assessment may not be validated—tested for validity, reliability, and objectivity prior to its use as a test to measure the performance of students. This and other concerns were the reasons Oscar Buros developed the *Mental Measurement Yearbook* in 1938. Buros' message was that formal tests should be used with caution. It is also the reason that Clinton Chase stated that it is wrong to use formal test alone. Clinton Chase, Oscar Buros, and others know that there is an error in all measurement and that all tests have limitations.

REVIEWING THE OPINIONS OF STAKEHOLDERS ON ACHIEVEMENT TESTING

In Chapter five, many viewpoints of professional education organizations as well as other stakeholders are presented. There seems to be many areas of consensus between the views of professional education organizations and lay stakeholders such as parents on the topic of achievement testing. Parents have often arrived at their viewpoints because they want the best possible education for their children. Generally, parents' positive and negative experiences with their own children in school settings have caused them to form the viewpoints that they hold.

On the other hand, professional education organizations arrive at their viewpoints through actual practice, study, and research. Professional education organizations have members at different levels and areas of the educational continuum from early childhood education to higher education and from the educational aide to the administrator. However, whether college professors, administrators, public and private elementary and secondary teachers, teacher researchers, or researchers, they all engage or have engaged in teaching and/or administration at various educational levels that are affected by achievement testing. Additionally, they have been exposed to pertinent research as practitioners or as participants.

Probably none of the stakeholders disagree with the desired outcome of education nor with the expectations of teaching and learning. The desired outcome of most parents for their children is that learning and experiences in school and supporting agencies will produce well-rounded, productive citizens who are lifelong learners. While the desired student outcome by educators is much the same as that of parents, the educators are constantly concerned with the optimal way to achieve the desired student outcome. They constantly ask themselves what is the optimal way of presenting a concept or subject so that it will be clear, understandable, and lead to permanent learning. More importantly, teachers/educators want to help each student develop independence in his/her content area that will lead to continued motivation and enthusiasm for learning when he/she is no longer in the classroom or in school.

Teachers pursue the goal of creating learners who have permanent knowledge and the capacity and flexibility to incorporate new knowledge into their schemes of thinking and their lives. The desired end is to create a learning environment which stimulates learning so that students "learn to learn" and are, therefore, ready for the academic, social, technological, and the myriad of local and global challenges of the twentieth-first century. Further, it is hoped that students' school experiences will help them be participants in the complex, shrinking global world. This participation is likely to occur if students possess the tools of critical, creative thinking; have awareness of many complex issues; know how to secure information and to use research; and have the interest, drive, and motivation to be problem solvers.

As mentioned above, there is a consensus among stakeholders as far as the desired educational outcomes and the expectations of the learning environment. There, too, are commonalities among professional education organizations as far as learning theories and assessment. These commonalities are found in the expression of their standards and position statements, summarized in Chapter five. Further, most of these organizations believe that it is necessary to examine their practices periodically to make sure that they are aligned with current research, the needs of stakeholders, learning theory, and optimal teaching and learning strategies. The National Assessment of Educational Progress did such an examination, such an audit. The highlights of the examination are presented by the editors Pellegrino, Jones, and Mitchell (1999) in *Grading the Nation's Report Card—Evaluating NAEP and Transforming the Assessment of Educational Progress* as described briefly in Chapter five.

Among the commonalities in learning theories and assessments are:

- The encouragement of active, participatory, integrated, student-centered strategic learning;
- The use of collaborative and cooperative learning which provide opportunities for students to share and weigh ideas as part of their growth and development in the "real" world;
- The development and incorporation of prior knowledge, reading, writing, discussion as well as higher-order thinking skills in all content areas;
- The recognition that culture as well as interest, motivation, attitudes, and multiple intelligences are extremely important considerations in all learning;
- The belief that multiple tools should be used to integrate and expand student learning. They should include such things as textbooks, newspapers, supplementary materials, trade books, out-of-grade-level books such as a picture books at any age. Computers should be used at all levels and in all content areas;
- The belief that no single measure or method of assessment of minimum competencies should ever be the sole criterion for graduation or promotion of a student. Multiple indices assessed through a variety of means, including teacher observation, student work samples, past academic performance, and student self-reports should be employed to assess competence. (This is a quotation from the International Reading Association, (cited by Valencia and Pearson (1987) in article "Reading Assessment: Time for a Change" in the April 1987 edition of The Reading Teacher), but it is aligned with the position of the major professional education organizations.)

There are other areas of consensus. The above areas do outline a number of commonalities. However, the current use of assessment shows a disregard for stakeholders and their opinions and past and contemporary research.

REEXAMINING SOME CRITICAL VARIABLES— SOCIOECONOMICS, UNIQUENESS OF LEARNERS, AND LIMITATIONS OF ALL TESTS— THAT AFFECT STUDENTS' TEST RESULTS

In re-examining the critical variables of socioeconomics, the uniqueness of learners, and the limitations of all tests, it should be noted that these critical factors are seldom discussed when presenting the results of achievement tests.

Socioeconomics

Diversity, especially in the area of socioeconomics, became a very important variable in the schools with the advent of the twentieth century when America began its move away from educating the elite to educating all American children. This move was reinforced by compulsory school attendance which was in effect in all states by 1918. Even with America's nearly-a-century-old move to educate all Americans, this is not a reality. Statistics from ERIC Clearinghouse on Urban Education for 1999 show a total dropout rate of 11.2 percent, 7.3 percent for whites, 12.8 percent for Blacks, and 25.6 for Hispanics. In many large cities, however, the dropout rate for minorities may be as high as 45 to 50 percent. (U.S. Department of Education 1999, 2003)

The road to equity in education has been rocky for many urban and rural socioeconomically poor children. The poor are often in jeopardy in our society and in schools since poor children not only live in poor homes that are situated in poor neighborhoods or communities, they usually go to poorly funded schools. Many African Americans are in double jeopardy because they are poor and because of their race. At the end of the nineteenth century and the beginning of the twentieth century when America was moving away from the education of the elite to a more inclusive model of education, African Americans were excluded by law. *Plessy v. Ferguson* (1896) established the practice of separate but equal in all public accommodations including the schools. This *de jure* segregation ended in 1954 when the United States Supreme Court ruled in *Brown v Board of Education of Topeka, Kansas* (1954), that separate but equal was inherently unequal and, therefore, unconstitutional. After 1954, *de facto* segregation became commonplace. As a consequence, the practice of *de facto* segregation exploded into a litigation battleground. This was evidenced by the numerous lawsuits against this unconstitutional practice in the 1960s, 1970s, 1980s, 1990s. The battleground in 2001and beyond is for equity in funding. Recently, many states have lost lawsuits in their state supreme courts for having inequity in school funding.

Looking at American's history, there is little wonder why poor children are generally found at the bottom of most standardized test result scales. When comparing family income and scores on the Scholastic Aptitude Test (SAT), the College Board Research Library of the Educational Testing Service's 1999 investigation supports the above statement. The sample of three categories of incomes and tests scores show: students who lived in a family which had an annual income of less than $10,000 had a combined verbal and math score of 873; students who lived in a family which had an annual income of $60,000 to $70,000 had a combined verbal and math score of 1040; students who lived in a family which had an annual income of more than $100,000 had a combined verbal and math score of 1142. Achievement test score findings, including the pervasive state proficiency tests, would also support this. What this picture vividly depicts is that money determines educational access in America. (Kantrowitz, 2001) Alfie Kohn (2000) said this very eloquently in his book, *The Case Against Standardized Testing* (2000):

> Anyone who is serious about addressing the inequalities of American education would naturally want to investigate differences in available resources. A good argument could be made that the fairest allocation strategy, which is only common sense in other countries, is to provide not merely equal amounts across schools and districts, but more for the most challenging student populations. (p. 38)

Certainly, the resources or lack of them and the inequity in school funding and other inequities such as segregation are critical variables in looking at the various achievement test performances of the socioecomically poor. While these factors are often overlooked, they greatly affect standardized achievement test scores.

UNIQUENESS OF LEARNERS

As pointed out in earlier chapters, especially Chapter seven, without recognizing that students learn in various ways, that they need to have opportunities to be taught using multiple approaches, and that they should be assessed by informal, authentic, and formal tests, America will, by design, be leaving " . . . some students behind." Certainly, some students may be learners whose learning approaches may be similar to those of Albert Einstein, Abraham Lincoln, Woodrow Wilson, Thomas Edison, Amelia Earhart, and others who were misevaluated in school but later recognized as America's heroes/heroines and/or geniuses.

Like the aforementioned heroes/heroines and/or geniuses, the talents of many of today's students may not be recognized or nurtured if multiple approaches of teaching, learning, and testing are not included in educational planning to salute the genius in all children. This is a key variable that is often overlooked in achievement testing, especially in "one-size-fits all testing." This certainly seems to be a consideration in the proposal of Richard Atkinson, president of the University of California (UC), which is to no longer require the aptitude portion of the Scholastic Aptitude Test (SAT) which is part I of the SAT. " . . . instead, he wants UC to adopt a more 'holistic' approach, which would consider (student) activities and grades, as well as scores on the SAT Part

II, the tests that measure mastery of particular subjects." This topic was presented by Barbara Kantrowitz and Donna Foote (2001) in an article dated March 5, 2001, entitled "The SAT Showdown" in *Newsweek* and an article by Diane Jean Schemo (2001) in February 17, 2001, issue of *The Plain Dealer* entitled "U. of California President Wants to Quit Using SAT."

LIMITATION OF ANY ASSESSMENT

The standard error of measurement is based on two concepts, the reliability of a test and how a score varies when compared with the scores of other students who have taken the test in the validation process. (Reliability is discussed in Chapter three.) Scores from any assessment may be thought of as having two parts. One is the true score; the second part is the error in any measurement. The limitations reflect the fact that every test has errors in it; no test is perfect, nor does any test assess everything related to a specific content area. These errors may come from varied sources. Only a few examples are presented here. Errors may occur from the inclusion of items containing vocabulary or concepts that have not been taught or that are above the developmental level of the student being tested. Errors may occur when a student guesses at an item and gets it correct or when a student responds incorrectly to an item that he/she knows. As mentioned above, the standard error of measurement is based on the reliability of a test.

Through thorough test validations, which determines the crucial measures of reliability and validity, many possible errors may be eliminated or avoided. However, such questions or items on untaught material are unfair to that student or students rather than being the typical error. Other items that may be unfair are items that are biased for or against a group of students. Albert Harris and Edward Sipay (1990) point out an area of general unfairness that has been discussed throughout this book. In their 1990 edition of *How to Increase Reading Ability*, they point out that, "Differences in educational experiences lead to differences in knowledge and the skills that tests are designed to measure. Our society does not provide equal educational opportunities for all. Eliminating or reducing average tests score differences might conceal this situation, but will not rectify it." (p. 192) Harris and Sipay's statement reinforces the idea that learning and testing should be integral. Equally as important is the understanding that no single test should be treated as if it is perfect.

CONDITIONAL STATEMENTS ABOUT THE USE OF ACHIEVEMENT TESTING

Achievement testing is an integral part of learning. It has always been a staple of teaching whether in school, in church, or at home. Many of the traditional forms have stayed the same. For example, observation, the essay test, and authentic assessment have been tools of education since the beginning of the teaching-learning process. Of course, the modern-day essay has been changed and improved with the addition of rubrics and checklists. And, authentic assessment has expanded. It is the expanded form of achievement test which is fairly new to educational assessment. Using a combination of assessments—self, informal, authentic, and formal—helps to create a holistic picture of the students' achievement. The main reason for using a combination of assessments is that no assessment is perfect. Additionally, a single assessment cannot provide a complete picture of a student.

Achievement testing is here to stay; however, all achievement testing should be used in a holistic way and with care and adherence to the directions, the design, and the research findings on the assessment. For this reason the following conditional statements can be made here.

- Achievement tests—formal, informal, and authentic—should be used if the test designer as well as the teacher/administrator, when a different person, has an awareness of the history and purpose of multiple types of assessments as well as their limitations.
- Achievement tests should be based on the goals and objectives of a particular content area and include multiple experiences which tap varied learning styles and modalities of learning of students.
- Educators/teachers should construct informal tests or assessments only after they have studied the ways of developing and weighing the validity, reliability, clarity, objectivity, and fairness of items.
- Educators/teachers should select formal tests only if they are well versed in the crucial area of test validation.
- Formal tests should be used only if they are highly valid and reliable and represent items and learning experiences that students have had an opportunity to learn and master.
- Formal tests should be selected with great care and only after stakeholders have reviewed the test on their own as well as consulted an objective external source such as the Mental Measurement Yearbook or Test Critiques.
- Key stakeholders should be major decision makers rather than legislators whose decisions may be made primarily for monetary or political reasons.
- Achievement testing results should become the focus for intervention and professional development that are not only designed to help students to master needed concepts but to provide teachers with new approaches and methods. The test results should also provide teachers and learners with insights into research and practice on multiple learning modalities and multiple intelligences.

- Norm-referenced tests or any form of assessment used to compare the performance of a student or class with students of the same age or grade level—the norm group—should be used only if the group being compared to the norm group has had the same educational experiences and opportunities as the norm group. As Albert Harris and Edward Sipay and others point out, "Our society does not provide equal educational opportunities for all."

- All stakeholders should be aware of the history of our country where equality of educational opportunity was denied African Americans by law until 1954 and by fact and inequity of funding until current times. Inequity of funding also affects American children who happen to be poor. Equality of educational opportunity should include needed interventions for those students who, as victims of the system, are "at risk" of educational failure. The plans and research have already been done for the needed intervention. Entwisle, Alexander, and Olson (1997) in *Children, Schools, and Inequality* and many other texts and professional education organizations have outlined workable intervention plans. Lisbeth Schorr in the 1989 edition of *Within Our Reach* has said that America knows how to stop poor school outcomes: now we must develop the will to do this.

- Assessment should be used as a tool of education only when it reflects the best learning, teaching, testing practices, and research. Further, assessment usage should reflect the unanimous view of leading education organizations that in unison and with assurance stated that no single assessment should be used to make major decisions such as students' passing from grade to grade or graduating from high school. Rather, major decisions should be based on multiple assessments which represent different types of experiences.

IMPLICATIONS

Achievement testing has always been part of teaching and learning. It has, however, expanded as the needs of the nation, the growth of student population, and new research findings occurred. As a result of these occurrences, schools in America began to move from educating a homogeneous population, that consisted of a few elite students, to educating the heterogeneous majority population that represents the nation's diverse elementary and secondary school-age children. Achievement testing in the expanded schools of the latter part of the nineteenth century and the entire twentieth century not only included forms of the teacher-made informal assessments of the early schools but a repertoire of tests that incorporated formal, authentic, and other assessments. In addition to the multiple types of achievement testing and the inclusion of "all of America's children," schools have changed in other ways. They have moved from places where the major stakeholders were just the parents and the teacher, as in the old one-room schoolhouse, to places where the stakeholders not only include the teacher and parents but administrators, community leaders, education organizations, politicians, legislators, the media, and others. The major goals of schools remain that of preparing students for higher education, the world of work, responsible citizenship, and options of family membership. Achievement testing is only one tool that helps in the attainment of these school goals.

In the burgeoning, new schools of the twentieth and twenty-first centuries, the formal test, which is a little over a century old, was and still is both a blessing and a curse. It is a blessing because it is objective and economical as far as the teacher's time and school district's spending. Additionally, it allows a student's performance to be compared to his/her previous performances during the school year, and from year to year; it also permits student groups to be compared from class to class, from school to school, from district to district, and throughout a state and the nation. On the other hand, it is a curse because some past as well as current test designers and many test consumers look at the formal test as perfect. They fail to consult research, best practices, standards of education organizations, and reference tools such as the *Mental Measurement Yearbook,* that evaluates, critiques, and publishes findings as well as warnings about formal tests. Further, many test designers and test consumers fail to factor into the test results the concept of the standard error of measurement; test limitations; basic learning, teaching, and testing goals and objectives; past and present inequities in funding and educational opportunities; and other critical variables. In many cases, these oversights have led to test unfairness, misuse and abuse, and even to a call for a moratorium on standardized intelligence and achievement tests by the National Education Association in 1972. (Perrone, 1977)

The features of the formal test design that make them objective, economical, and comparable are the reasons that formal tests have gained wide use and acceptance. These features are attractive and useful in large schools and for a nation that espouses to educate all children. For these reasons, formal tests are here to stay. Even with the staying power of the formal test, however, tests should be viewed as evolving—tools that need constant revision in order to meet the ever-changing needs of students and schools; tools that need modification in order to be aligned with educational goals, objectives, and national standards, and tools that need oversight to ensure the incorporation of research findings and best testing practices. Additionally, any test should only be administered to students when they have been exposed to the concepts on the tests and have had time to master them and when the test complements class work and other assessments—formal, informal, authentic, and even the teacher's observation. A critical component of any test must be the motivating, viable, and available intervention that moves the student to mastery on the tested concepts. Since we say that children are unique, we must have assessments that tap their uniqueness—based on the concepts of divergent and convergent thinkers as well as the theories of multiple intelligences. Further, a study of American history and state and national laws reflects the fact that America has failed to distribute educational funds and other opportunities equally among all segments of the population. Contrary to history and research, our current use of formal high-stakes tests says that all students learn the same way—they are not unique—that all students have had equal educational opportunities, and that formal tests are error free and without limitations. These assumptions are far from true. Any test is just a sample of the tested concepts and student behavior. Many samples are needed to get a whole academic picture of a student. For all of these reasons, it is critical that test designers and test consumers view any test with skepticism, that multiple types of assessments be used, and that all stakeholders remember that no assessment—formal or other—is powerful enough to make up for lack of educational opportunity.

REFERENCES

Adkins, D. C. (1974). *Test Construction*. Columbus, OH: Charles E. Merrill, A Bell & Howell Company.

Anastasi, A. (1976). *Psychological Testing*. New York: Macmillan.

Barnes, J. E. (March 22–29, 2004). "Unequal Education" in "50 Years After Brown." *U.S. News & World Report*, 136(100: 66–75.

Barr, R. and Johnson, B. (1991). *Testing Reading in Elementary Classrooms*. White Plains, NY: Longman.

Barr, R. and Parrett, W. (1995) *Hope at Last for At-Risk Youth*. Boston: Allyn and Bacon.

Beatty, A. S.; Greenwood, M. R. C.; Linn, R. L. (1999). "Myths and Tradeoffs—the Role of Tests in Undergraduate Admissions." The Report of the 1999 Investigation of the College Board of the Educational Testing Service by the National Research Council of the Academy of Sciences. Washington, DC: National Academy Press.

Brown v. Topeka Board of Education, Kansas, Shawnee County. (1954). 374 U.S. 483.

Buros, O. K. (1938–2003). *The Mental Measurement Yearbooks*. Highland Park, NJ: Gryphon Press (1938–1978). Lincoln, NE: University Nebraska Press (1985-2003).

Entwisle, D. R.; Alexander, K. L.; Olson, L. S. (1997). *Children, Schools, & Inequality*. Boulder. CO: Westview Press.

Ewers, J. (March 22–29, 2004) "Making History" in "50 Years After Brown." *U.S. News & World Report*, 136(10):76–80.

Foner, E. and Garraty, J. (1991). *The Reader's Companion to American History*. Boston: Houghton Mifflin.

Harris, A. J. and Sipay, E. R. (1990). *How to Increase Reading Ability: A Guide to Developmental and Remedial Reading*. New York: Longman.

Kantrowitz, B. and Foote, D. (March 5, 2001). "The SAT Showdown." *Newsweek*, 48–50.

Keyser, D. J. and Sweetland, R. (eds.) (1984–1994). *Test Critiques*. :Kansas City, MO: Test Corporation of America 1984–1988). Austin, TX: Pro?Ed (1991-2003).

Kohn, A. (2000). *The Case Against Standardized Testing: Raising the Scores, Ruining the Schools.* Portsmouth, NH: Heinemann.

Manzo, A.V. (May 2003). "Literacy Crisis or Cambrian Period? Theory, Practice, and Public Policy Implications." *Journal of Adolescent & Adult Literacy*, 46(6): 654–667.

Pellegrino, J. W.; Jones, L. R.; Mitchell, K. J, (eds.). (1999). *Grading the Nation's Report Card: Evaluating NAEP and Transforming Assessment of Educational Progress.* Washington, DC: National Academy Press.

Perrone, Vito. (1977). *The Abuses of Standardized Testing.* Bloomington. IN: Phi Delta Kappa Educational Foundation.

Plessy v. Ferguson (1896). 163 U.S. 537.

"Professor Says Poor Schools Don't Get Fair Share of Funds." (November 22, 1993). Cleveland, OH: *Plain Dealer, B3.*

Schemo, D. J. (February 17, 2001). "U. of California President Wants to Quit Using SAT." Cleveland, OH: *The Plain Dealer.*

Schorr, L. B. with Schorr, D. (1989), *Within Our Reach: Breaking the Cycle of Disadvantage.* New York: Anchor Books, Doubleday.

U.S. Department of Education, Institute of Education Science. (1999) (2003). *Condition of Education Report: Status Dropouts: Dropout Rates of 16-to 24-year-olds, By Race/Ethnicity: October 1971–2001.* Washington, DC: National Center for Education Statistics.

U.S. News & World Report. (March 22–29, 2004). "50 Years After Brown." 136(10): 65

Valencia, S. and Pearson, P. D. (April 1987). "Reading Assessment: Time for a Change."[Position Statement of the International Reading Association included.] *The Reading Teacher. 40:726– 732.*